BEFORE CHRIST CAME

HIGHWAY TO HEAVEN SERIES

BOOK OF THE HOLY CHILD (Grade One)

LIFE OF MY SAVIOR (Grade Two)

LIFE OF THE SOUL (Grade Three)

BEFORE CHRIST CAME (Grade Four)

THE VINE AND THE BRANCHES (Grade Five)

THE MISSAL (Grade Six)

HIGHWAY TO GOD (Grades Seven and Eight)

Accompanying this Series is the RELIGION IN LIFE CURRICULUM for grades one to six and PRACTICAL PROBLEMS IN RELIGION for grades seven and eight.

HIGHWAY TO HEAVEN SERIES IV

Before Christ Came

BY A SCHOOL SISTER OF NOTRE DAME
*of the faculty of St. Paul Diocesan
Teachers College, St. Paul, Minn.*

St. Augustine Academy Press
Homer Glen, Illinois

Nihil obstat:
R. G. BANDAS,
Censor librorum

Imprimatur:
✠ JOANNES GREGORIUS MURRAY,
Archiepiscopus Sancti Pauli

April 7, 1933

ACKNOWLEDGMENTS

The author hereby makes grateful acknowledgment to the following: Rev. Rudolph G. Bandas, S.T.D. et M., Professor of Dogmatic Theology, St. Paul Seminary, Rev. Wm. McGucken, S.J., St. Louis University, Rev. Wm. Griffin, D.D., Mapleton, Minn., Rev. Alton H. Scheid, Chaplain, Good Counsel Academy, Mankato, Minn., for reading of manuscript and helpful suggestions; to the School Sisters of Notre Dame for their generous encouragement and help; and finally to Dr. Edward A. Fitzpatrick, Editor of the Highway to Heaven Series, whose splendid efforts in behalf of religious education have inspired this little volume.

This book was originally published in 1934 by The Bruce Publishing Company. This edition reprinted in 2017 by St. Augustine Academy Press based on the 1935 second printing.

Softcover ISBN: 978-1-64051-030-2
Hardcover ISBN: 978-1-64051-031-9

My dear young readers:

The story of what men and women have done in the world is divided into two parts. The event that marks the division is the birth of Christ. This is in fact the greatest event in the history of the world. You will learn more later about how Christ's coming down from heaven into the world has had many, many effects down to our own day and will go on to the end of time. Today, more than nineteen hundred and thirty years after the birth of Christ, He is the greatest influence for hundreds of millions of people in the world.

In this book we go back to the time "before Christ came," particularly among the Jewish people, the chosen people of God. In those old days they had and kept the knowledge of the one true God. To them He made the promise of a Savior or Redeemer, who was Christ, our Lord. He would come surely. They expected Him. The prophets told about His coming, though they did not know the exact time. They told long before He came that He was to be born in Bethlehem in a manger. He would be born of a virgin. He would suffer greatly even to crucifixion. He would rise again from the dead.

This great and wonderful story is told in this book

in a very interesting way. Learn that story in all its details. Memorize the prophecies. Study carefully the problems asking you to tell what you would do if you were in the place of the person described in the problem. In these and in the other problems use good judgment. Do so in your home, on the street and playground, and in the schoolroom. Show your love of God by using good judgment. Show your love of your neighbor by using good judgment.

If you have some free time all for yourself, use it on the "good things to read" and "the interesting things to do" that are given in this book.

By all means talk over all these things with your father and your mother. Tell them about your use of good judgment. After you have decided what to do about the problems in the book, talk it over with them. Ask them what their "good judgment" would be. Ask them what they would do if they were in the place of the person described in the problems in this book.

After reading how the people of Israel waited for centuries for the coming of our Lord, be happy that every month, or better every week, He will come to you, if you wish, and that you will look forward expectantly and joyfully for His coming.

EDWARD A. FITZPATRICK

CONTENTS

	PAGE
INTRODUCTION	v
Unit I. GOD'S BEAUTIFUL, WONDERFUL WORLD	1
1. The Holy Bible	2
2. How God Made the World	5
3. God's Garden on Earth	10
4. The Sin of God's People	11
5. God's Wonderful Promise	13
6. Cain Becomes a Wanderer	18
7. Rain for Forty Days	23
8. A Rainbow in the Sky	25
Unit II. THREE LEADERS OF GOD'S PEOPLE	29
9. The Land of Promise	30
10. A Priest of the Most High God	34
11. Three Guests Come to Abraham	37
12. The End of Two Cities	43
13. Abraham Obeys God's Voice	44
14. Rebecca at the Well	49
15. Esau Sells His Birthright	54
16. The Hunter Returns	58
17. A Dream of God	60
18. Jacob Meets Rachel	63
19. Forgiveness	66
20. Joseph, the Dreamer	71
21. Sold as a Slave	75
22. The Forgotten Prisoner	79
23. Go to Joseph	81
24. The Famine Comes to Chanaan	86
25. Back Again to Egypt	88
26. The Missing Cup	94
27. The Return of Good for Evil	96
28. A Father Finds His Long-Lost Son	98
29. Jacob Blesses His Children	100
30. A Man Whom God Loved	102
Unit III. MOSES, THE GREAT LAWGIVER	107
31. A Princess Finds an Infant Boy	109

	PAGE
32. Called by God	111
33. Egypt is Punished with Plagues	117
34. Walking Through the Red Sea	121
35. God Sends Food from Heaven	128
36. God Gives the Ten Commandments	131
37. The Israelites Worship a Golden Calf	133
38. Scouting in the Land of Promise	136
39. Water from a Rock	143
40. The Death of a Great Leader	145
Unit IV. JOSUE AND THE JUDGES	149
41. Back in the Land of Promise	151
42. Gedeon, the First of the Judges	153
43. A Faithful Daughter	159
44. The Lord Speaks to a Child	166
Unit V. ISRAEL RULED BY KINGS	171
45. The First King of Israel	172
46. A Shepherd Boy Becomes King	177
47. David Kills a Giant	179
48. David Sings of the Redeemer	182
49. A King Who Asked for Wisdom	185
Unit VI. GREAT PROPHETS OF ISRAEL	191
50. Elias is Fed by the Ravens	192
51. Eliseus Cures Naaman, the Leper	197
52. A Good Father's Teachings	202
53. On a Journey with an Angel	205
54. A Prophet Tells of the Redeemer	211
55. Jeremias Weeps Over Jerusalem	213
Unit VII. THE BABYLONIAN CAPTIVITY	215
56. A Captive Prophet	217
57. Daniel in the Den of Lions	219
58. Saved by a Queen	223
59. A Woman of Courage	230
Unit VIII. WAITING FOR THE KING	237
60. The Last Great Leader	239
61. He Is Coming	241
62. Preparing the World for the Redeemer	242
PRAYERS	248

UNIT I
God's Beautiful, Wonderful World

Would you like to know how God made this beautiful, wonderful world of ours? The first eight stories of this book will tell you about the beginning of the world and the first people that lived in it. They will also tell you how God loved His people of the earth and how it happened that He made a wonderful promise to them.

1. The Holy Bible

The most wonderful book that was ever written is the Holy Bible. It tells us about the beginning of the world and our first parents, Adam and Eve. It also tells us about the sin of our first parents and God's promise of a Redeemer.

For four thousand years God's people remembered the wonderful promise which He had made to them. Often they turned away from Him and prayed to false gods. Sometimes they fell into the hands of their enemies and had to suffer a great deal. But God loved His people and watched over them. As soon as they turned back to Him again, He was ready to help them. Through all the years they watched for the Redeemer and prayed that He would come and save them. Holy men, called prophets, told many things about Him long before He came. They said that He would be the Son of God; that He would do great wonders; and that He would suffer and die for them. All this we are told in the first part of the Holy Bible, called the Old Testament.

At last the Redeemer came. We are told about Him in the second part of the Holy Bible, called the New Testament. In this part we learn what the Redeemer taught and what great wonders He worked for the

So the heavens and the earth were made.

people whom He loved. We read that they would not believe in Him and at last put Him to death; that He arose again from the grave and sent His Apostles out to preach to the whole world. We also learn of the work and the writings of the Apostles and their followers.

The word "Bible" means "the Books." If we examine the Holy Bible, we shall see that it is really not one book at all. It is made up of smaller parts, each one of which is called a book by itself. Altogether there are seventy-two books in the Holy Bible. Forty-five books belong to the Old Testament and twenty-seven to the New Testament. The books of the Holy Bible are not like other books. Although they were written by men in words which we can all read, they are the Word of God. That means that the people who wrote these books were guided by the Holy Ghost to say just what God wanted us to know. That is why the Holy Bible is the most wonderful book in the whole world.

We cannot read all of the Holy Bible now, but we shall want to read it later on, as we grow older. We shall want to read the stories exactly as they were written many years ago. Our book tells us some of the stories of the Old Testament. We shall see how the hope of the Promised Redeemer runs all through them like a golden thread. Because these stories were written so long ago, the words and sentences in them will sometimes sound different from those which we find in other books. But we shall love them all the more, because they are the words of the Holy Bible, and God's message to us, His children.

* * *

Now answer the following questions:
1. Which is the most wonderful book that was ever written?
2. About whom does the Old Testament tell us?
3. About whom do we learn in the New Testament?
4. What does the word "Bible" mean?
5. How many books are there in the Holy Bible?
6. Who guided the people that wrote the Holy Bible?
7. Why should we love the stories of the Holy Bible?

2. How God Made the World

The story of the Creation is told in that wonderful book, the Holy Bible, about which we have read in the first lesson. Read the story carefully in order that you may learn how God made heaven and earth and all things, and how people first came to live in this beautiful world of ours.

In the beginning there was nothing but God alone. God had no beginning and will have no end. He always was and always will be.

On the first day God made heaven and earth. The earth was dark and empty. There was neither sun nor moon: there were no trees, no flowers, no animals, and no people.

Then God said: "Be light made." And light was made. And He called the light Day and the darkness Night. That was on the first day.

On the second day God said: "Let there be a firmament made, and let it divide the waters from the waters." And God called the firmament Heaven.

God spoke again on the third day and said: "Let the waters that are under the heaven be gathered together into one place and let dry land appear." And God called the dry land Earth, and the water He called the Sea. And God said: "Let the earth bring forth green plants and the fruit tree bear fruit." And it was done.

And on the fourth day God said: "Let there be lights made in the firmament to divide the day and the night."

And God made two great lights: the sun to rule the day and the moon to rule the night: and then the stars. And He set them in the firmament to shine upon the earth.

God spoke on the fifth day: "Let the water bring forth fish and creatures of all kinds, and birds that may fly over the earth." And He blessed them saying: "Increase and multiply and fill the waters of the sea! and let the birds be multiplied upon the earth."

On the sixth day God said: "Let the earth bring forth living creatures, cattle and creeping things, and the beasts of the earth." And it was done.

Last of all God said: "Let Us make man to Our image and likeness." And He made the first man and woman. Then He blessed them and said: "Increase and multiply and fill the earth."

So the heavens and earth and all things were made. And God saw that they were good.

On the seventh day God rested from all His work which He had done. He blessed the seventh day and made it holy.

* * *

Now answer the following questions:
1. Who made God?
2. Did God ever have a beginning?
3. What did God create on the second day?
4. On what day did God create the fish and the birds?
5. What did God create the last of all?
6. What did God do on the seventh day?
7. Is there anything that God did not create?

Read the story again to see whether you have all the answers correct.

When God made man, He gave him a body and a soul. Therefore man is a creature composed of body and soul and made to the image and likeness of God.

Using good judgment:

When people choose the very best way of saying or doing a thing, we say that they use good judgment. Read over the following little problems and then try to show good judgment by choosing the best answer.

1. Paul is a little dark-skinned boy who lives in your neighborhood. He seems to be very well behaved, but all the boys and girls laugh at him and make fun of him because he came

to this country only a short time ago and cannot speak English very well. Do you think the children should treat him as they do? There are three reasons given below why Paul should be treated as kindly as any of the other children. Which of the three reasons do you think the best?

Paul ought to be treated kindly because:
 a) He might get angry and hurt you.
 b) God made him and loves him just as much as He loves other children.
 c) He feels hurt because everybody laughs at him.

2. God made many beautiful things and gave them to us to use and enjoy. We ought always to be very careful not to harm any of God's wonderful gifts. Can you tell some ways in which boys and girls can show good judgment and care in using lawns, flowers, trees, birds, and toys?

How to make a character book:

Take four sheets of ruled tablet paper and fold them carefully in the middle. With a needle and strong white thread sew the pages of the book together in the middle where the pages are folded. On the outside of your book write your name and the words "My Character Book."

In this book you may write little poems and sentences which you wish to remember. They will help you to become better every day. They will help you to please God and to become a blessing to your home, your school, and your country.

From the following sentences and short poems choose those which you think will help you most to become good men or women. Be sure to use good judgment.

I must always consider the rights of other people.

I must be careful not to harm any of God's creatures, such as trees, birds, animals, or flowers.

I must be careful to show respect to all people, whether

they are rich or poor, whether they speak my language or not. I will try to look for beautiful things wherever I go.

When I notice something very beautiful, like a lovely flower, a bright butterfly, or a glorious sky, I will remember to thank God for all the beautiful things He made.

> "The world is so full of a number of things
> I'm sure we should all be as happy as kings."
> — *Stevenson*

> Know ye that the Lord He is God:
> He made us and not we ourselves.
> We are His people
> And the sheep of His pasture.
> (Ps. 99)

More things for you to do:

1. Find a picture of beautiful flowers, birds, fruit, or trees, and with it make a poster. Write on the poster such words as: "God's gift of flowers," "God's gift of fruit," etc.

2. Make a list of all the creatures you can think of that God created on each of the six days of creation. Divide your paper into six columns, one for each day.

3. Make a Creation Booklet, using a page for each day of creation. Find pictures of the particular creation for each day and paste them into your booklet.

4. Find as many poems as you can, that tell something about God's beautiful world. Read or recite one of the poems to the class.

5. If you like to draw, make a picture to show what God created on each particular day of creation and copy from the story the words that belong under each picture.

6. Memorize the following sentence which is taken from the Holy Bible: "In the beginning God created heaven and earth."

7. Say the Apostles' Creed. Which sentence tells about the creation?

* * *

Can you answer these questions?
1. Who made the world?
2. Who is God?
3. Had God a beginning and will He have an end?
4. Who made you?
5. Why did God make you?
6. How can you show that you love God?
7. How can you serve God?
8. Where is God?
9. Why can we not see God?

3. God's Garden on Earth

When God made Adam and Eve, He wanted them to live in the earthly Paradise first, and afterwards to be happy with Him in heaven. Had they remained good and obedient, they and all the people that came after them, would never have had to die. Then there would have been no pain or sorrow in this world. But God wanted our first parents to prove their love for Him by their obedience to His law. In the following stories we shall see what God did to test the love and obedience of Adam and Eve and how they stood the trial.

When God created Adam, He put him into a beautiful garden called Paradise. There He brought before

Adam all the animals He had created. Adam gave names to all the beasts, and all the birds of the air, and all the cattle of the field. But in spite of the lovely garden and all the animals, Adam was lonely, because there was no one there like himself.

Therefore God said: "It is not good for man to be alone: let Us make him a helper like unto himself." Then He sent a deep sleep over Adam, and when he was fast asleep, God took a rib from his side and formed the body of a woman.

When Adam saw the woman whom God had made for him, he was very happy. He said: "This now is bone of my bone and flesh of my flesh: she shall be called woman because she was taken out of man."

This woman was named Eve, which means "mother of all the living."

4. The Sin of God's People

The Paradise in which Adam and Eve lived had everything to make them happy. There were birds and flowers and trees of all kinds.

One day God said to Adam: "Of every tree of Paradise you shall eat. But of the tree of knowledge of good and evil, you shall not eat. For if you do eat of it, you shall die the death."

Now, one time when Eve was walking in the garden looking at the lovely fruit God had given them, the devil

The devil in the form of a serpent spoke to Eve.

in the form of a serpent spoke to her from one of the trees and said: "Why did God command that you should not eat of every tree of Paradise?"

Eve answered: "We do eat of the fruit of the trees that are in Paradise. But of the fruit of the tree which is in the middle of Paradise, God has commanded us that we should not eat, lest perhaps we die."

But the serpent said: "No, you shall not die the death, but your eyes shall be opened, and you shall be as God, knowing good and evil."

Eve believed the serpent. She took of the fruit and ate, and also gave her husband to eat. Then the eyes of their souls were opened so that they could know good and evil, and they knew that they had done wrong.

5. God's Wonderful Promise

When Adam and Eve saw what they had done, they were ashamed and sad and they hid themselves among the trees. God called Adam and said to him: "Where are you?"

Adam answered: "I heard Your voice in Paradise. I was afraid, and I hid myself."

Then Adam told God that it was the woman who gave him the fruit to eat, and God said to Eve: "Why have you done this?"

She answered: "The serpent deceived me and I did eat."

And the Lord told the serpent that because he did this, he would be cursed among all the cattle and beasts of the earth: and would creep on his breast and eat earth all the days of his life. And He spoke these words to the serpent: *"I will put enmities between thee and the woman, and thy seed and her seed: she shall crush thy head, and thou shalt lie in wait for her heel."*

God sent Adam and Eve out of the beautiful Paradise.

And to Adam He said: "Because you have listened to the voice of your wife, and have eaten of the tree of which I commanded you not to eat, the earth is cursed in your work: you shall eat with labor and toil all the days of your life. It shall bring forth thistles to you: and you shall eat the plants of the earth. In the sweat of your face you shall eat bread till you return to the earth out of which you were taken: for dust you are and into dust you shall return."

Then God sent Adam and Eve out of the beautiful Paradise and put an angel with a flaming sword at the gate, so that they could never again come back. Poor Adam and Eve! They went away very sad, but they knew that God did not punish them forever. When He said the words: *"I shall put enmities between thee and the woman"* He meant to tell them that some day He would send a Redeemer who would open for them the gates of heaven which were now closed on account of their sin. That was a wonderful promise. Adam and Eve always remembered it. They often spoke about it to their children and told them never to forget that some day God would keep His promise and send them a Redeemer.

Now answer the following questions:

1. What was the beautiful garden called in which Adam and Eve lived?
2. Who gave the animals their names?
3. Why was Adam lonely in Paradise?
4. How did God make the first woman?
5. What is the meaning of the name "Eve"?
6. Why did Eve eat of the forbidden fruit?
7. What did the serpent tell Eve?
8. Did the serpent's words come true?
9. How did Adam and Eve feel after they had eaten of the fruit?
10. How did God punish the serpent?
11. How did God punish Adam and Eve?
12. Was heaven closed forever after the sin of Adam and Eve?
13. With what words did God promise a Redeemer?

God has given His laws to us also and we must obey them. Do you know any laws that God has given us?

Using good judgment:

Find the best answer:

1. John goes into a store and finds a beautiful jackknife lying on the counter where he can easily take it without being seen. John should not take the knife
   a) Because he might be caught by the police;
   b) Because his father might find out and punish him;
   c) Because God commands us not to steal.

2. Bonnie's mother wishes to visit some friends and tells Bonnie to stay at home for the afternoon to take care of the baby. The baby has just gone to sleep and usually sleeps for two hours. Bonnie has promised her chum next door to come over and see her new kittens. Should she go while the baby is asleep? What is the reason for your answer?

3. Suppose you had been in Paradise and the serpent had told you what he told Eve. What would you have done? Why?

More things for you to do:

1. Imagine that you are Adam or Eve and that their children are all around you asking for a story. Tell them about the beautiful garden you used to live in, about the tree in the middle of Paradise, and what happened after you ate the fruit. Let them ask you questions. Be sure to tell them especially about God's promise to send a Redeemer and to remind them that they and their children should always remember that promise and watch for the coming of the Redeemer.

2. Make a sand-table project of the garden of Paradise.

3. Make a clay model or drawing of one of the animals of Paradise.

4. Draw or cut out the Tree of Knowledge with the serpent wound around it. Tell the story.

5. Study by heart the promise of a Redeemer God made in Paradise to Adam and Eve.

6. Write in your character book: When I am tempted to do wrong, I will pray, "Jesus, help me!"

7. Write a little story about some children who were disobedient and were very sorry after they saw what happened.

8. Can you find the blank into which these words fit: Adam, Eve, heaven, Redeemer, serpent, God, Paradise, tree, fruit?

a) The first man and woman were .... and ....

b) They lived in a place called ....

c) God told them they should not eat of the fruit of one .... which stood in the middle of Paradise.

d) Eve took .... from the forbidden tree and ate it.

e) The .... tempted Eve to take the fruit.

f) .... punished Adam and Eve by sending them out of Paradise.

g) The sin of Adam and Eve closed not only Paradise but also ....

h) God promised to send Adam and Eve a ....

Good things for you to read:

"The Garden of Paradise," *A Child's Garden of Religion Stories*, Matimore, page 9.

"Tried and Found Faithful," *Ideal Catholic Reader*, Book IV, page 164.

"The Carrier Pigeons," *Ideal Catholic Reader*, Book IV, page 201.

"The First Rain," *American Cardinal Reader*, Book IV, page 171.

Can you answer these questions?

1. Of what is man composed?
2. Who were our first parents?

3. Why were Adam and Eve punished?
4. What is sin?
5. Was heaven closed forever after the sin of Adam and Eve?

6. Cain Becomes a Wanderer

God told Adam and Eve that they would have to suffer much pain and sorrow on account of their disobedience. As soon as they left Paradise, their sufferings began. They had to find food and shelter, and they had to protect themselves against all kinds of danger. We shall now learn of a great sorrow that Adam and Eve had to bear on account of one of their children.

Two sons were born to Adam and Eve. Their names were Cain and Abel. Cain was a farmer and Abel a shepherd. One day the two brothers went out to offer a sacrifice to God. Cain offered of the fruits of the earth and Abel of the best of his flock. God was pleased with the offering of Abel, who was good and kind, but he was not pleased with the offering of Cain because he was jealous and hard-hearted. Therefore Cain became very angry.

The Lord said to him: "Why are you angry? If you do well, will you not receive good from Me? But if you do evil, you will be punished. Control your wicked desires and you will overcome them."

One time Cain said to Abel, his brother: "Let us go

CAIN BECOMES A WANDERER 19

Cain struck his brother Abel and killed him.

out into the field." And when they were out in the field where no one could see them, Cain struck his brother Abel and killed him.

But the Lord said to Cain: "Where is your brother Abel?"

He answered, "I do not know. Am I my brother's keeper?"

Then God said: "Cain, what have you done? The voice of your brother's blood cries to Me from the earth. Therefore you shall be cursed, and the earth shall not bring forth its fruit for you. You shall be a wanderer all your life."

And Cain said to the Lord: "My sin is too great for me to be forgiven. I must hide myself from Your face and everyone that finds me will kill me."

But the Lord said to him: "No, it shall not be so: Whoever shall kill Cain, shall be punished."

And He put a mark upon Cain, that whoever found him should not kill him. And Cain went away and lived as a wanderer on the east side of Paradise.

Now answer the following questions:
1. Why did Cain kill Abel?
2. What did Cain offer to God as a sacrifice?
3. With whose sacrifice was God pleased?
4. What did God ask Cain after he had killed Abel?
5. What did Cain answer?
6. How did God punish Cain?
7. What does it mean to control one's self?

The following are all examples of self-control. Read the rules over and see whether you keep them all. Try to be honest with yourself.

I must always play fair.

I must never lose my temper.

I must never use the name of God or of holy things in anger.

When others are praised I must try to overcome all feelings of jealousy and be glad with them.

I must be a good sport when I lose in a game or contest.

I must take correction or punishment with a good will.

I must always be pleasant and courteous to others, whether I feel like it or not.

I must never use improper language.

I must not quarrel with my little sisters and brothers nor with my playmates or classmates.

CAIN BECOMES A WANDERER 21

Copy in your character book all those rules which you think you ought to remember and practice.

What would you do if you were in their place?

1. John and Charles are classmates. John is praised by the teacher for a good lesson. Charles thinks that John has not deserved the praise and that the teacher is just saying those things because she likes him. What would you call such thoughts? Is it wise for Charles to keep such thoughts in his mind? Suppose Charles told you how he felt, what would you say to him?

2. Dan received a prize in school for the best language lesson. Fred knows that Dan did not do the work himself but had an older boy do it for him. If you were Fred, what would you do?
   a) Tell the teacher all about it.
   b) Tell all the pupils what you know about it.
   c) Talk to Dan about it.

3. Marie and her friend play a game. Marie loses. She gets angry and refuses to play another game. If you were Marie, what would you do?
   a) Stop playing and show that you are angry.
   b) Say that your friend cheated.
   c) Tell your friend that she played a good game and then try again.

4. Your little brother always wants your toys. Mother says that you should let him play with them. You are afraid he will break them. What should you do?
   a) Throw down the toys and go away angry.
   b) Scold your little brother and slap him.
   c) Play with him and show him how to use the toys.

5. You are in church, ready to go to confession. A boy comes in and pushes ahead of you. Should you:
   a) Run ahead of the boy.

b) Control yourself and keep quiet.

c) Kick him and make a face at him.

6. Father promised to take Will out to a basketball game one evening. When the time came Will's father could not leave the office. What would you expect Will to do?

a) Cry over his disappointment.

b) Ask his mother to leave her work and take him to the game.

c) Be a good sport and plan to go another time.

7. Ellen brings home a friend for the evening. Ellen's sister Marie does not like the friend. What should she do?

a) Go upstairs and read all evening.

b) Help Ellen make things pleasant for her friend.

c) Leave the house and go somewhere else to play.

8. The teacher corrects Tom for cheating. Tom can best show self-control by

a) Taking the teacher's correction to heart and making up his mind not to cheat again.

b) Denying his fault and answering back.

c) Telling his mother that the teacher picks on him.

More things for you to do:

1. Choose two members of your class to give a little play to show how the loser can be a good sport in a game, such as marbles.

2. If you have a sand table, build a project showing the two stone altars which Cain and Abel probably made for their sacrifice.

Good things for you to read:

"Suppose," Phoebe Cary, *Ideal Catholic Reader,* Book IV, page 107.

"Clara's Roses," *Cathedral Basic Reader,* Book IV, page 22.

Can you answer these questions?

1. What should Cain have done when he noticed his evil thoughts against Abel?
2. What sin did Cain commit?
3. Could Cain's sin have been forgiven?
4. Did Cain ask God to forgive him?
5. How can our sins be forgiven?

7. Rain for Forty Days

Adam and Eve had many children. Some of them lived to be very old. The Holy Bible tells us that Adam lived to be nine hundred and thirty years old and Seth, one of his sons, lived to be nine hundred and twelve years old. Seth was a good and holy man. He and his children remembered the wonderful promise which God had made to Adam and Eve in Paradise, and looked for the coming of the Redeemer. As long as the children of Seth obeyed him, they remained good and happy. But by and by they began to marry some of the children of Cain, who did not wish to know and serve God. Soon the world became a very wicked place, where people forgot all about God. In the story of Noe you will learn how God punished the wicked people of the world because they would not love and serve Him.

When God saw how wicked men were, He said: "I will destroy man, whom I have created, from the face of the earth."

But there was one man and his family who still

Noe built an ark out of wood.

served God. That man was Noe. God told Noe to build a large ark or boat, because soon He would send a flood to destroy the people of the earth. Noe did as he was told. He built an ark out of wood and covered it with pitch so as to keep out the water. When the work was finished, God told him to bring into the ark a pair of every kind of animal that lived on earth and also food for them and for his family. When everything was ready, Noe and his wife and his sons with their wives went into the ark and God Himself closed the doors behind them.

Then for forty days and forty nights the rain fell upon the earth until everything was covered with water. The ark alone with all that were in it floated on the water and was saved.

8. A Rainbow in the Sky

The great flood filled the earth for one hundred and fifty days. Then God thought of Noe and all that were with him in the ark. He sent a warm wind over the earth and the waters sank lower and lower until at last the ark stood still on the top of a mountain.

Noe waited for forty days and then opened the window of the ark and sent out a raven. The raven did not return. Then he sent out a dove, but the dove could not find a place to rest and came back to the ark. After seven days Noe again sent out the dove, and it returned with an olive branch in its mouth. He waited seven days more and once more sent out the dove. This time it did not return. Then Noe opened the ark and saw that the earth was dry. God said to him: "Go out of the ark and bring with you all the living things upon the earth."

When all were upon the dry earth again, Noe built an altar of stone and offered a sacrifice of thanks to God. The Lord was pleased with the sacrifice and blessed Noe and his sons, saying to them: "Increase and

As a sign of His promise He placed a rainbow in the sky.

multiply and fill the earth." Then He promised that He would never again destroy man with a flood, and as a sign of His promise He placed a rainbow in the sky.

From that time on the children of Noe spread over the whole earth.

Now answer the following questions:
1. Why did God send the great flood?
2. How long did it rain?

3. Who were saved from the flood?
4. What did Noe take into the ark?
5. How did Noe try to learn if the land was dry?
6. Why did the dove come back the first time it was sent out?
7. What was the first thing Noe did after he left the ark?
8. What promise did God make to Noe?
9. What sign did God give to Noe to remind him of His promise?

When people saw Noe building a large boat where there was no water, they laughed at him. But Noe believed God's words. He knew that God watches over those that love Him and trust in Him. He did not mind what other people said, because he knew that he was doing right.

Say an act of Faith, Hope, and Charity, to tell God that you believe what He says, and that you trust Him and love Him. Be sure to think of the meaning of the words.

It is a good thing for every Catholic to make acts of Faith, Hope, and Charity, every day.

Can you tell how Noe showed his faith in God's word, his hope and trust in God's help, and his love and gratitude for all His goodness?

Interesting things for you to do:

1. Learn by heart one of the following poems:
"The Rainbow," C. Rosetti.
"The Rainbow," John Keble.
"The Song," Robert Loveman, *Literature for Reading and Memorization*, Book IV, page 105.

2. In your character book write at the top of the page the word "Gratitude." Find a quotation or short poem about gratitude and copy it in your character book.

3. Dramatize The Building of the Ark, or Noe's Sacrifice.
4. Make a sand-table project of Noe and the ark.

5. Make a drawing or poster of a rainbow. Learn the rainbow colors; violet, indigo, blue, green, yellow, orange, red (vibgyor).

6. Make a list of all the animals you think went into the ark.

7. Learn the following quotations which are taken from the Holy Bible. Tell how these words fit into the story of Noe.

"The fear of the Lord is the beginning of wisdom. Fools despise wisdom and instruction" (Prov. i. 7).

"My son, hear the instruction of thy father, and forsake not the law of thy mother" (Prov. i. 8).

Good things for you to read:

"Rain Poems," *Child Story Readers,* Book IV, pages 104–107.

"Drifting in the Flood," *A Child's Garden of Religion Stories,* Matimore, page 20.

"The Man Whom God Spared," *The Bible Story,* page 12.

Can you answer these questions?

1. Why did Noe believe God when He said He would send a flood?

2. How did Noe know that God could save him and his family?

3. How did Noe offer sacrifice to God?

4. How do we offer sacrifice to God?

5. What is the Mass?

6. When must a Catholic go to Mass?

7. What else should a Catholic do on Sundays? What should he not do?

UNIT II
Three Leaders of God's People

When God chooses people to do great things for Him, He sometimes tries them to see whether they obey and trust Him and whether they love Him above all things.

In the following stories we shall see how God tried the great men whom He had chosen as the leaders of His people and the founders of a new nation. We shall see also how they stood the test of God's love and how He rewarded them.

9. The Land of Promise

A long time after the great flood there lived in Haran a good and holy man whose name was Abram. Because Abram served God with all his heart, he was loved by the Lord, who said to him: "I will make you a great nation, and I will bless you. I will bless them that bless you, and curse them that curse you, and all the nations of the earth shall be blessed in you." God also told him that he would no longer be called Abram, but Abraham, which means "the father of the multitude."

One day God told Abraham to leave Haran and go into the land that He would show him. Abraham, therefore, took Sara, his wife, Lot, his brother's son, and also his servants and many flocks and herds, and left the country in which he lived. When Abraham and his family came near the city of Bethel, in the land of Chanaan, they pitched their tents and offered a prayer to the Lord.

By and by a famine came into Chanaan, and Abraham went down to the land of Egypt until it was over. Then he returned to Bethel once more and offered prayers to the Lord.

Now, Lot had many sheep and herds and tents of his own. And the servants of Lot quarreled with the servants of Abraham because there was not enough pasture for all the animals. Therefore Abraham said to Lot: "Let there be no quarrel between you and me, and between your servants and my servants: for we are

THE LAND OF PROMISE

brethren. Behold, the whole land is before you. If you choose the land to your left, I will go to the right: and if you choose that to your right, I will go to the left."

Lot looked around and saw that the country on the Jordan River was the richest and most beautiful: and he chose it as his own. Then he left Abraham and went to live in the city of Sodom which was a very wicked place.

After Lot had left, the Lord said to Abraham: "Lift up your eyes and look to the north and to the south, to the east and to the west. All the land which you see, I will give to you and to your children forever." Because God made this promise to Abraham, the land of which He spoke was called Land of Promise.

Now see whether you can answer the following questions:

1. Why did God bless Abraham?
2. What did Abraham do when he came to the Land of Chanaan?
3. Why did Lot's and Abraham's servants quarrel?
4. How did Abraham settle the quarrel?
5. Where did Lot go to live after he left Abraham?
6. What promise did the Lord make to Abraham after Lot had left him?

As soon as Abraham arrived in the Land of Promise, he gave thanks to God. In this way he showed how thankful he was for all that the good God had done for him.

Name as many people as you can, who do good to you. To how many of these do you ever say, "Thank you"?

Watch yourself today and say "Thank you" for all the little kindnesses that others do to you.

Abraham had a right to take the best land for himself. But he was unselfish. He told Lot to choose first the land that he wanted.

What would you do if you were in their place?

1. Jack has two apples, one bigger than the other. He is saving one for mother. If he is unselfish, which apple will he give her?
2. If Jack wanted to give his little sister one of the apples and keep the other for himself, which should he give to her?
3. If Jack's mother had two apples of different sizes and she let him choose, which one should he take?

Do you know of any boys or girls who are unselfish and do not always take the best for themselves?

Do you show selfishness at home? Watch yourself today, to make sure that you do not ask for the best of everything.

Write in your character book those of the following sentences which you would like to remember for yourself:

I will say "Thank you" for even the smallest kindness others show to me.

I must be as polite at home as I am in company.

I must work and play with others without quarreling.

I must be polite and patient when helping others.

I must be careful not to choose the best for myself.

More things for you to do:

1. Dramatize little acts of kindness children can do for others and show how one should act when receiving a kindness.
2. Make a poster or drawing using the words, "I must be polite."
3. Write a little story about an unselfish boy or girl.
4. Tell some stories about Jesus and how He showed His unselfishness and His kindness to others.

THE LAND OF PROMISE 33

5. Find little stories about animals that have shown themselves grateful for a kindness and tell the class what you have read.

6. Find little poems or quotations that tell about unselfishness or politeness.

7. Memorize the following poem:

SOMEBODY

Somebody did a golden deed;
Somebody proved a friend in need:
Somebody sang a beautiful song;
Somebody smiled the whole day long;
Somebody thought, "'Tis sweet to live":
Somebody said, "I'm glad to give":
Was that somebody you?

Good things for you to read:

"Reward of Obedience," *De La Salle Reader*, Book IV, page 105.

"Abraham," *Ideal Catholic Reader*, Book IV, page 86.

"The Faithful Abraham," *A Child's Garden of Religion Stories*, pages 31–37.

"The Miraculous Pitcher," *Cathedral Basic Reader*, Book IV, page 177.

Can you answer these questions?

1. How can we thank God for His goodness?
2. Why was it not right for the servants of Lot and Abraham to quarrel?
3. Why should children not quarrel?
4. What is meant by selfishness?

10. A Priest of the Most High God

At one time four kings came upon Sodom, the place in which Lot and his family lived. They robbed the city and captured the people. Among those who were captured were Lot and his wife with all that belonged to them. When Abraham heard what had happened, he took three hundred and eighteen of his men and followed the enemy. He rushed upon them during the night, defeated them, and brought Lot and all the other people that had been captured back to their homes.

On the way home Abraham met Melchisedech, the King of Salem, who was a priest of the Most High God. Melchisedech offered a sacrifice of bread and wine to God. Then he blessed Abraham and said: "Blessed be Abraham by the Most High God, who created heaven and earth. Blessed be the Most High God who gave the enemies into your hands."

Abraham then gave to Melchisedech a tenth of all that he had taken. The King of Sodom was so thankful to Abraham for defeating the enemy, that he wanted him to keep all that he had taken from them. Therefore he said: "Give me the people that you have captured and keep all the other things for yourself."

Abraham, however, answered: "I will not take any of the things that belong to you." He would not accept anything from the people of Sodom because they were very bad.

A PRIEST OF THE MOST HIGH

Melchisedech offers wine and bread.

Now can you answer the following questions?

1. Who was Melchisedech?
2. What offering did he make to God?
3. What did Abraham give to Melchisedech?
4. What did the King of Sodom want Abraham to keep?
5. What did Abraham answer?
6. Why would he not take anything from the King of Sodom?

The sacrifice of Melchisedech reminds us of the sacrifice of the Mass. Melchisedech took bread and wine and offered it to God. During Holy Mass the priest takes bread and wine and changes it into the Body and Blood of Jesus Christ.

Abraham showed respect to Melchisedech because he was a priest of the Most High God. He gave to the priest a tenth of all he had. We also must show great respect to our priests, because they take the place of Jesus Christ on earth. We must also help them by contributing to the support of the church and by otherwise being good children of our parish.

Are you a good child of your parish?

A good Catholic child:
1. Attends Mass every Sunday and holyday of obligation.
2. Goes to the sacraments regularly.
3. Brings an offering to church every Sunday if he can.
4. Honors and obeys his priests and teachers.
5. Goes to a Catholic school so that he can learn his religion well.
6. Is proud of his religion.
7. Knows that his religion is the best gift God has given him.

A good Catholic boy tips his hat when he passes a Catholic church.

A good Catholic girl bows her head when she passes a Catholic church.

Copy the sentence you like best into your Character Book.

Interesting things for you to do:

1. Cut out or draw pictures of all the articles used at the Holy Sacrifice of the Mass.
2. Make a list of the things a priest does for us.
3. Make a list of the things you can do to help the priest and your church.
4. A little boy asks you why you raise your hat when you pass by the church. Write what you would tell him.
5. Dramatize the sacrifice of Melchisedech.

Good things for you to read:

"The Mass," *American Cardinal Reader*, Book IV, page 112.

"The 100% Good Turn," *American Cardinal Reader*, Book IV, page 237.

"St. Philip's Lesson," *Wonder Stories of God's People*, Matimore, page 338.

"When You Go to Holy Mass," *The Catholic Youth Reader*, Book IV, page 230.

"How the Church was Built," *Misericordia Reader*, Book IV, page 318.

Can you answer these questions?

1. Of what great sacrifice does the offering of Melchisedech remind you? Why?
2. Who said the first Mass?
3. When was the first Mass said?
4. What does the priest do at Mass?
5. What should you do during Mass?
6. Which are the principal parts of the Mass?
7. What is the name of your church?
8. What can you do to help support the church?
9. Why should people help to support the church?

11. Three Guests Come to Abraham

One day as Abraham was sitting by the door of his tent, he saw three men coming toward him. He arose at once and went to meet them. As soon as they came nearer, he saw that it was the Lord. He bowed low and said: "Lord, if I have found favor in Your sight, go not away from Your servant. While You rest under the tree, I will bring some water to wash Your feet, and then I will bring food so that You may be strengthened."

And they answered: "Do as you have said."

Abraham went into the tent and told Sara to take flour and make some cakes. Then he himself ran out

Abraham stood by to serve his guests.

to the herd, picked out a tender calf, and gave it to a servant who prepared it for the visitors.

When the meal was ready, Abraham brought out butter and milk and set the food before them. Then he stood near by so that he could serve them.

When they had eaten, they said to him: "Where is Sara, your wife?"

He answered: "She is in the tent."

Then the Lord promised Abraham that he would come again in a year and that Sara would by that time have a son.

Now, Sara was in the tent listening to what the Lord said. She laughed to herself when she heard that they were to have a son, for although they had long prayed for one, she and Abraham were now old and no longer expected God to give them children. But the Lord knew that Sara was laughing and said: "Is there anything hard for God? I shall be back in a year, and then Sara shall have a son."

From Abraham's tent the three guests turned toward the city of Sodom, and Abraham walked with them part of the way.

Good things for you to read:

"A Little Hypocrite," *Cathedral Basic Reader,* Book IV, page 48.

"The Basque Song," *American Cardinal Reader,* Book IV, page 84.

"Imelda, the First Communicant," *The Catholic Youth Reader,* Book IV, page 372.

"Jesus Rewards His Beloved," *A Child's Garden of Religion Stories,* page 250.

"A Child's Wish," Abraham J. Ryan.

Now answer the following questions:

1. Who were the three guests that came to Abraham?
2. How did Abraham treat them?
3. What food did Abraham serve to the visitors?
4. Where was Abraham while they ate?
5. Where was Sara during the meal?
6. What did the Lord promise to Sara?
7. Why did Sara laugh?
8. What did the Lord say when He saw that Sara did not believe Him?

If the Lord came to your house, what would you do for Him? Has the Lord ever come to you? When? What do you do to entertain Him? How often do you invite the Lord to come to you?

When you entertain Jesus, the Divine Guest, are you careful about the following?

Before Communion:

1. Be sure you have no mortal sin on your soul.
2. Go to confession if you have a mortal sin on your soul.
3. Do not eat or drink anything from midnight on.
4. Prepare your soul for the coming of Jesus:
    a) Think of Jesus and talk to Him,
    b) Tell Him you love Him,
    c) Tell Him you are sorry for your sins,
    d) Tell Him you want Him to come to you.

At Holy Communion:

1. Go to the rail with hands folded and eyes down.
2. All the time keep thinking of Jesus.
3. When your turn comes, raise your head and put out your tongue.

THREE GUESTS COME TO ABRAHAM 41

4. Swallow the Sacred Host as soon as you can.
5. Walk back to your place slowly and do not look around.

After Holy Communion:

1. Remember Jesus is in your heart.
2. Tell Him again how much you love Him.
3. Tell Him you are glad He came into your heart.
4. Tell Him about yourself, your lessons, your sins, your little secrets.
5. Ask Him to bless your parents, your teachers, and your friends.

And Remember:

1. Do not leave the church for at least ten minutes after Holy Communion.
2. Use your prayer book if you cannot think of more to say.
3. Never touch the Sacred Host with the fingers. If it sticks to your mouth, loosen it with your tongue and swallow it.
4. Invite Jesus to come to you soon again.

Study the following little poem and say it often before you go to Holy Communion:

> Jesus, Jesus, come to me,
> Oh, how much I long for Thee.
> Thou of all the friends the best,
> Take possession of my breast.

Can you answer these questions?

1. What is Holy Communion?
2. What is necessary to make a good Communion?
3. Is any one ever allowed to receive Holy Communion without fasting?
4. How often must we receive Holy Communion?
5. How often may we receive Holy Communion?

Fire came down and destroyed the wicked cities.

12. The End of Two Cities

As Abraham walked along the road to Sodom with his three guests, the Lord told him that He would destroy the two cities Sodom and Gomorrah because the people had become very wicked. Abraham felt sorry for the people and hoped he could save them from punishment. Therefore he said to the Lord: "If there are fifty good persons in the city, will you not spare the people for the sake of the fifty?" And the Lord said: "If I find only fifty in Sodom, I will spare the whole place for their sakes."

Abraham asked again: "What if there are five less than fifty persons, will you destroy the city?"

And again the Lord answered: "I will not destroy it if I find five and forty who are just."

Again and again Abraham asked the Lord the same question, each time naming a smaller number. At last he said: "If there are only ten good people in the city, will you not spare it for their sakes?"

And the Lord answered: "If there are only ten just in Sodom, I will spare the city."

But when the angels came to Sodom, they did not find even ten good people. Only Lot and his family had remained true to the Lord. Therefore the angels told Lot to take his wife and two daughters at once and leave the city without stopping to look back. Hardly were Lot and his family out of the gates, when fire came from heaven and destroyed the two wicked cities. Lot's wife did not obey the command of the angels. She turned around and looked back at the burning city. Therefore she was at once turned into a statue of salt.

Now answer the following questions:
1. What were the names of the two wicked cities?
2. Why did Abraham ask the Lord to spare the people?
3. Were there ten good people left in Sodom?
4. Who were the only good people in the city?
5. What did the angels tell Lot to do to save himself and his family?
6. How did the Lord destroy the city?
7. What happened to Lot's wife after she left the city?

God punished the cities of Sodom and Gomorrah on account of their wickedness. God hates sin and punishes those who offend Him. We must be very careful not to commit sin, especially mortal sin. We are guilty of mortal sin when we commit a great wrong against God's law. When the wrong we commit is not so great, it is a venial sin.

Tell Jesus how sorry you are for the sins that you have committed. Say an act of contrition and be sure to think of what you are saying.

13. Abraham Obeys God's Voice

God remembered His promise to Abraham and Sara and sent them a little boy whom they called Isaac. They watched over their son as only good parents can, and loved him more every day. God knew how much Abraham loved Isaac. He wished to see whether he

ABRAHAM OBEYS GOD'S VOICE

loved the boy more than he loved God. Therefore He said to Abraham one night: "Take your only begotten son Isaac, whom you love, and offer him for a sacrifice on one of the mountains which I will show you."

Abraham got up in the night, saddled his donkey, and took with him two servants and Isaac his son. And when he had cut wood for the sacrifice, he started on his way to the place which God pointed out to him. On the third day he saw the mountain from afar off, and said to his servants: "Stay here. I and the boy will go on, and after we have worshipped, we will return to you."

Then he took the wood for the sacrifice and laid it on Isaac's shoulders, while he himself carried fire and a sword.

Isaac said to his father: "My father, we have fire and wood; but where is the victim?"

And Abraham answered: "God will provide a victim, my son."

So they went on together until they came to the place which God had shown him. Here Abraham built an altar, and when he had bound Isaac, his son, he laid him upon the altar on the wood. Then he raised the sword in his hand to sacrifice his son.

But an angel of the Lord called him saying: "Abraham, Abraham, do not lay your hand upon the boy, neither do anything to him. Now I know that you fear God and have not spared your only begotten son for My sake."

When Abraham looked around, he saw a ram caught

Abraham laid Isaac upon the altar.

ABRAHAM OBEYS GOD'S VOICE

by the horns in a bush near by. He took the ram and offered it instead of his son.

And the angel of the Lord called Abraham a second time and said: *"In your seed shall all the nations of the earth be blessed because you have obeyed My voice."*

With these words the Redeemer was promised once more. Because Abraham showed his great love for God by being willing to sacrifice his son, God promised that the Redeemer should come out of his family.

Now answer the following questions:

1. Why did God try the obedience of Abraham?
2. What did He tell Abraham to do?
3. What did Abraham take with him for the sacrifice?
4. Did Isaac know that his father would sacrifice him?
5. Who stopped Abraham when he was about to sacrifice Isaac?
6. What did he offer instead?
7. What promise was made to Abraham on account of his obedience?

Imagine that you are Abraham and that your son Isaac is asking you about the meaning of the words that the angel spoke: "In your seed shall all the nations of the earth be blessed because you have obeyed My voice." Explain the meaning to Isaac and show him how God had made the promise of the Redeemer long, long before in Paradise. Tell him the story of the disobedience of Adam and Eve and repeat the exact words of God's promise to them. Be sure to make Isaac understand how important it is for him to remain true to God and to watch and pray for the coming Redeemer just as Adam and Eve and their children had waited and prayed for Him.

More interesting things for you to do:

1. Dramatize the story of Abraham and Isaac.
2. Isaac is a type of Jesus. That is, he was like Jesus in many ways. See whether you can finish the following sentences by showing in what ways they were alike:

   a) Isaac was the only son of his father; Jesus was the only son of ....

   b) Isaac carried the wood of the sacrifice on his shoulders; Jesus carried the heavy ....

   c) Isaac went up to the mountain to be sacrificed; Jesus went up to ....

   d) Isaac was bound by Abraham; Jesus was bound by the wicked ....

   e) Isaac was obedient to the will of his father; Jesus said, "Father, not My will ...."

Perhaps you can find more ways in which Jesus and Isaac were alike.

Can you answer these questions?

1. By what prayer do we tell God we are sorry for our sins?
2. When should we make an act of contrition?
3. If Isaac had been sacrificed by his father, would the sacrifice have been as great as the sacrifice of Jesus on the cross? What is the difference?
4. Who is Jesus Christ?
5. How many persons are there in God?
6. Why did God promise a Redeemer?

Good things for you to read:

"Abraham Proves His Love," *A Child's Garden of Religion Stories,* page 47.

"Abraham's Obedience," *The Bible Story,* page 25.

14. Rebecca at the Well

Abraham was now getting old; he wanted to see Isaac married before his death. But as the women of Chanaan did not believe in the One True God, he called Eliezer, one of his servants, and said: "Go to my people in my own country and there choose a wife for my son Isaac."

Eliezer took ten camels and many rich presents and started out for Haran, Abraham's early home. When he arrived before the city, it was evening, and he stopped to rest at a well where the women came to get water. Here Eliezer prayed: "O Lord, show kindness to my master Abraham. I stand near the spring where the daughters of this city will come to draw water. I shall say to a maid: 'Let down your pitcher that I may drink.' And if she shall answer, 'Drink, I will give your camels to drink also,' I shall understand that she is the one whom You have chosen as the wife of Isaac."

Hardly had he said these words, when a beautiful girl came with a pitcher on her shoulder. She went down to the well to fill her pitcher, and when she was coming back, Eliezer stopped her and said: "Give me a little water to drink from your pitcher."

She answered: "Drink, my Lord." And she quickly let down the pitcher on her arm and gave him to drink. When he had drunk, she said: "I will draw water for your camels also, until they all have to drink."

Rebecca gives water to Abraham's servant.

Eliezer watched her without speaking, and wondered whether the Lord had heard his prayer.

When the camels had all drunk their fill, Eliezer gave the girl golden earrings and rich bracelets and asked her: "Whose daughter are you? And tell me, is there any room in your father's house to stay overnight?"

She answered: "I am Rebecca, the daughter of Bathuel, who is a son of Nachor. We have a good store of both hay and straw and a large place in which to sleep."

Eliezer bowed down his head and prayed: "Blessed be the Lord God of my master Abraham, who brought me straight into the house of my master's brother."

In the meantime Rebecca ran home and told her mother all that had happened.

Now Rebecca had a brother named Laban who, when he had heard all that she told them, went out quickly to the well and said to Eliezer: "Come in, blessed of the Lord. I have prepared the house for you, and also a place for the camels." And he brought Eliezer into the house and set food before him.

But the servant said: "I will not eat until I have given you my message."

Laban answered: "Speak."

Then Eliezer told them about Abraham and his great riches, and how his master had sent him to find a wife for Isaac among the people of his own country. He also told them how he had prayed to God to show him who was to be the wife of Isaac, and how his prayer was answered when Rebecca came to the well.

When Laban and Bathuel had heard these words, they said: "This is the word of the Lord. We cannot do anything better than to please Him. Rebecca stands before you. Take her and go your way, and let her be the wife of your master's son, as the Lord has spoken."

Eliezer thanked the Lord, and gave them all rich presents.

The next morning Eliezer said: "Let me depart, that I may go to my master."

And they said: "Let us call the maid and ask her will."

They called her, and when she had come, they said: "Will you go with this man?"

She said: "I will go."

So Eliezer and Rebecca started on their way to Chanaan. There Rebecca became the wife of Isaac, who loved her very much.

Abraham lived to be one hundred and seventy-five years old. When he died, Isaac buried him beside his wife Sara, who had died some time before.

Now see whether you can answer the following questions:

1. Why did Abraham not want Isaac to have a wife from Chanaan?
2. How did Eliezer find out whom God had chosen for Isaac?
3. Who came to the well for water?
4. Who was Rebecca's father?
5. Who was Rebecca's brother?
6. When did Eliezer and Rebecca start for Chanaan?

7. How old was Abraham when he died?
Read the story over again and find out for what Eliezer prayed the first time. Did God hear his prayer? Why did he pray a second time?

Giving a play:

Choose one or more of the following titles and give a little play, pantomime, or tableau about them. Be sure to let the players say the prayers that fit into the play:
 Good Morning, Mother
 Children Saying Their Morning Prayer
 Children Saying Their Night Prayer at Mother's Knee
 A Family at Meals
 Children Begging God to Bless Their Studies
 Children Saved From Danger (Prayer in Danger)
 A Child's Prayer to the Guardian Angel
 My Jesus, Are You There (In the tabernacle)
 A Temptation That Didn't Work (Prayer in temptation)
 A Sorry Son (Contrition)
 Good Night

If you can find a little poem or hymn to fit into your play, be sure to use it.

Learn the following hymn:

> Jesus, teach me how to pray,
> Suffer not my thoughts to stray,
> Send distractions far away,
> Sweet, Holy Child!
> Let me not be rude or wild,
> Make me humble, meek and mild,
> Pure as angels undefiled,
> Sweet, Holy Child!

Copy the following Scripture text into your character book:
To Thee, O Lord, have I lifted up my soul. In Thee, O my God, I put my trust; let me not be ashamed (Ps. 24. 2).

Can you answer these questions?
1. What is prayer?
2. When should we pray?
3. How should we pray?
4. Does God always answer our prayers?

15. Esau Sells His Birthright

When the father of a family died in the days of Abraham and Isaac, the first-born or eldest son took his place as the head and priest of the family. This right of the first-born was known as the birthright. It gave to the eldest son not only a double share of the father's property, but also the right to the father's special blessing. With this special blessing the father handed over to the first-born son the promise of the Redeemer for whom every one was so eagerly waiting. We can now understand why, in the following story, the two sons of Isaac had such a bitter quarrel over their birthright.

Isaac and Rebecca had two sons, Esau and Jacob. Esau, the elder, was rough and strong and grew up to be a hunter. Jacob was quiet and gentle. He lived at home and raised sheep. Esau was Isaac's favorite, because his father liked to eat the food which he brought home from the hunt; but Rebecca loved the gentle Jacob.

One day when Jacob was boiling some pottage, Esau came home from the hunt weak and hungry. He said to

"Give me some of your pottage, for I am hungry."

Jacob: "Give me of your pottage, for I am very hungry."

Jacob answered: "Sell me your birthright, and I will give you to eat.

Esau said: "What good will my birthright do me if I die of hunger?" Then he sold his birthright to Jacob, ate and drank, and went away thinking no more about it.

The time came when Isaac grew old and blind. Therefore he called his son Esau and said: "You see I am old and do not know the day of my death. Go out with your bow and arrow, and when you have shot something, prepare a meal for me, such as you know I like, so that I may eat, and give you my blessing before I die."

When Esau had gone out, Rebecca called Jacob and said: "I heard your father talking with Esau and saying to him: 'Bring me of your hunting, that I may eat and bless you before I die.' Now, my son, listen to what I tell you. Go out to the flock and bring me two of the best kids, that I may prepare the meat for your father as he likes it, so that when he has eaten, he may bless you instead of Esau."

But Jacob answered: "You know that Esau is a hairy man, and I am smooth. If my father shall feel me and find out who I am, I fear he will think that I wished to mock him and curse me instead of giving me his blessing."

His mother answered: "Only listen to me. Go, fetch

ESAU SELLS HIS BIRTHRIGHT

me the things which I have said." Jacob went and brought the two kids to his mother, and she prepared the meat as Isaac liked it best. Then she dressed her favorite son in Esau's good garments and covered his bare neck and hands with the skins of the kids.

Jacob carried the food to his father and said: "My father!"

And Isaac answered: "I hear. Who are you, my son?"

Jacob answered: "I am Esau, your first-born. I have done as you commanded me. Arise, sit and eat of the food, and then bless me."

Isaac asked his son: "How could you find food so quickly, my son?"

He answered: "It was the will of God that what I was looking for came in my way so quickly."

And Isaac said: "Come here, that I may feel you, my son, and may prove whether you are my son Esau or not."

Jacob came near to his father, who, when he had felt him, said: "The voice, indeed, is the voice of Jacob; but the hands are the hands of Esau. And again he asked: "Are you my son Esau?"

He answered: "I am."

Then Isaac asked his son to bring him the food, and when he had eaten, he said: "Come near me, and give me a kiss, my son."

Jacob came near and kissed him.

Isaac then spoke the blessing over his son: "God give you the dew of heaven and of the fatness of the earth.

Let people serve you and tribes worship you. Be you the lord of your brethren and let your mother's children bow down before you. Cursed be he that curses you, and let him that blesses you be filled with blessing."

16. The Hunter Returns

Jacob had hardly left the tent, when Esau came with the meat he had prepared for his father and said: "Arise, my father, and eat of the meat I have brought you, that you may bless me."

And Isaac said to him: "Why! Who are you?"

He answered: "I am your first-born son, Esau."

Isaac was struck with fear and surprise. "Who is he then," he asked, "that even now brought me to eat? I ate before you came, and I have blessed him and he shall be blessed."

Esau cried aloud with disappointment when he heard his father's words. "Bless me also," he begged.

But Isaac said: "Your brother deceived me and got your blessing."

And Esau answered: "First he took away my birthright, and now he has stolen away my blessing. Have you only one blessing, father? Bless me also." And again he cried aloud.

Isaac felt sorry for his son, and blessed him also. But it was not the same blessing that Jacob had received.

From that time on Esau hated Jacob and wanted to kill him.

When Rebecca heard what Esau wished to do, she sent for Jacob and said to him: "Esau, your brother, wants to kill you. Go, therefore, to Haran, to my brother Laban and stay with him for a few days. When Esau is no longer angry and has forgotten what you have done to him, I will send for you again."

Now answer the following questions:
1. Who was the first-born son of Isaac?
2. What rights did the first-born son have?
3. Why was Esau the favorite of Isaac?
4. What did Isaac ask Esau to do for him?
5. Who got the blessing of the first-born?
6. How did Rebecca dress Jacob before she sent him to his father?
7. What did Esau want to do to Jacob for stealing the blessing from him?
8. Did Esau get the same blessing that Jacob got?
9. Where did Rebecca send Jacob?

When Esau sold his birthright to Jacob, he gave away a great gift. We are children of God. Heaven is our birthright. We sell our birthright when we commit mortal sin. Esau was foolish to sell that wonderful gift for something to eat. But are not we also foolish to sell heaven for the sake of some little thing we want?

Three things make a sin mortal:
1. The wrong we do must be very great.
2. We must know that what we are doing is a great wrong.
3. We must fully wish to do the wrong.

Tell the class different ways in which boys and girls can sell their right to heaven.

Can you answer these questions?
1. What is mortal sin?
2. What is necessary to make a sin mortal?
3. How can mortal sin be forgiven?
4. Can mortal sin ever be forgiven without confession?
5. To whom did Christ give the power to forgive sins?

17. A Dream of God

Jacob prepared to go to Haran, where Laban, his uncle, lived. Isaac blessed him once more and said: "Go to the house of your mother's father and there take a wife. God Almighty bless you and make you a great people. I give the blessing of Abraham to you and to those who come after you: that you may possess the land which He promised to your grandfather."

On his way to Haran, Jacob stopped to rest. At night he laid his head on a stone and fell asleep. While he was sleeping, he saw a ladder standing on the earth with its top touching heaven. On the ladder, angels were moving up and down and above was the Lord Himself. And God spoke to Jacob in his sleep and said: "I am the Lord God of Abraham and the God of Isaac. I will give the land on which you sleep to you and to your seed." Then once more He made the wonderful promise that He would send a Redeemer: *"In thee and thy seed all the tribes of the earth shall be blessed."*

When Jacob awoke, he said: "Indeed, the Lord is in

He saw a ladder with its top touching heaven.

this place, and I did not know it." And trembling, he continued: "How terrible is this place. This is no other but the house of God and the gate of heaven."

In the morning when Jacob arose, he took the stone on which he had laid his head, and blessed it, because he was now the priest of his father's family. Then he set it up as a sign that the place was holy. He called the place Bethel, which means House of God, and promised that if God would be with him and bring him safely back home, he would give a tenth of all he had to the Lord.

Now answer the following questions:
1. To whom did Jacob go when he left home?
2. What happened to Jacob while he was asleep?
3. What did Jacob call the place where the angels appeared to him on a ladder?
4. What promise did God make to Jacob?
5. What did Jacob promise to give if he came home safely?

Interesting things for you to do:
We call the church the House of God. Why do we call it by that name?
1. Choose a committee to write out for the class the rules for correct behavior in church. When the rules have been read and talked over by the class, let some of the pupils show how each action is to be done correctly and tell why we do it. For example, one of the pupils may show how to genuflect before the altar and then tell the class why a genuflection should be made.
2. Have one of the pupils prepare a little talk in which he tells what can be done by children to make the House of God beautiful.

Good things for you to read:

"The Little Lamp," *American Cardinal Reader,* Book IV, page 6.

"Correct Behavior in Church," *The Catholic Youth Fourth Reader,* page 343.

"The Chimes of St. Patrick's," *The Catholic Youth Fourth Reader,* page 346.

"A Church Underground?" *American Cardinal Reader,* Book IV, page 248.

"Esau and Jacob," *Wonder Stories of God's People,* page 3.

"The Lamp of the Sanctuary," *Catholic National Reader,* Book IV, page 139.

Can you answer these questions?

1. Who founded the Catholic Church?
2. Who is the visible head of the Church?
3. Where does he live?
4. What is the name of the present Pope?
5. Why do Catholics make a genuflection in Church?
6. How does Jesus come down on the altar?
7. Why does Jesus come down on the altar?
8. How should we behave in Church?

18. Jacob Meets Rachel

When Jacob came near to the end of his journey, he stopped at a well where the shepherds were gathered with their flocks, and asked them: "Where are you from?"

The shepherds answered: "From Haran."

Then he asked whether they knew Laban, and the

shepherds answered that they knew him and that Rachel, Laban's daughter, would soon come to the well with her father's sheep.

While they were still talking, Rachel came to the well. Jacob knew at once that she was his cousin and cried with joy at meeting her. He moved the stone away for her from the well, and after the sheep were watered, he told her that he was the son of Rebecca, her father's sister. Rachel ran home to tell her father, and when Laban heard that Jacob, his sister's son was near, he ran out to meet him and brought him into his house.

After Jacob had been at the house of Laban for some time, his uncle asked if he would stay and work for him. Jacob loved Rachel, the beautiful daughter of Laban, and answered: "I will serve you seven years if you will give me Rachel for my wife."

Laban answered: "It is better that I give her to you than to another man; stay with me."

Jacob stayed and served Laban for seven years, and they seemed but a few days, because he loved Rachel so much. When the seven years were over, he asked Laban to give him Rachel for his wife. But Laban did not keep his promise. He gave him Lia, his older daughter instead, because it was not the custom for the younger daughter to marry first.

Jacob, however, was angry and said to Laban: "Why did you deceive me? I asked for Rachel and you gave me her sister instead."

Laban answered: "Remain seven years longer in my

service and I will give you Rachel also." Jacob promised that he would remain and Rachel was also given to him as wife.

For twenty years Jacob worked at Haran and God blessed his labors, so that he became a rich man. Then He discovered that Laban was jealous of him. So he called his wives and children together and told them that the Lord wished them to go back to the land of Chanaan, where Isaac, his father lived. They left Haran secretly while Laban was away shearing sheep. When Laban found out that Jacob had left with his wives and all his flocks, he was very angry and followed after them. But God said to him in a dream: "Be careful that you do not speak in anger to Jacob."

After seven days Laban found Jacob on a mountain, and the two made peace with each other and offered sacrifice to God. Then Jacob went on his way to his father's house.

Now answer the following questions:

1. Where did Jacob first meet Rachel?
2. How long a time did he work for Laban to get Rachel as a wife?
3. Why did the time not seem long for him?
4. Whom did Laban give to Jacob as wife after the first seven years?
5. How long was Jacob at Haran?
6. Why did he leave Haran?
7. Was Laban pleased to have him go?
8. How did Laban and Jacob part?

19. Forgiveness

When Jacob drew nearer to the home of his father, he became very much afraid, and prayed to God: "O Lord, you told me to return to the place of my birth. Deliver me now from the hands of my brother Esau, for I am much afraid of him." Then he sent some of his servants ahead to meet Esau and offer him many presents.

During the next night an angel wrestled with Jacob. When morning came, the angel said: "Let me go, for it is break of day."

Jacob answered: "I will not let you go until you bless me."

"What is your name?" asked the angel.

He answered: "Jacob."

"You shall not be called Jacob any longer," the angel said, "but Israel, which means 'Strength of God.'" Then he blessed Jacob and disappeared. He meant to show Jacob that he did not need to be afraid of men, since he had been strong enough to wrestle with an angel of God.

That same morning Jacob saw his brother Esau coming toward him with four hundred men. Jacob went forward and bowed down with his face to the ground seven times, until his brother came near. Then Esau ran to meet Jacob and put his arms about his brother's neck and kissed him.

When Esau saw the women and children, he asked: "Who are these?"

His brother answered: "They are the children God has given me."

And they all came forward and bowed before Esau. Then Jacob gave him gifts of many camels, goats, sheep and other animals. Esau did not want to accept them, but Jacob said: "Take of the blessing which I have brought you and which God, who gives all things, has given me."

As a sign that he had forgiven his brother, Esau accepted the gifts from Jacob, and then returned by the way he had come. Jacob, however, went on with his journey until he arrived in the land of Chanaan, where Isaac, his father, lived. Here, at the age of one hundred and eighty years, Isaac died, and Esau and Jacob buried him.

Now answer the following questions:
1. Why was Jacob afraid to return home?
2. What happened to Jacob one night on his way home?
3. What name did the angel give to Jacob?
4. How did Jacob meet his brother Esau?
5. What did Esau do when he saw Jacob?
6. What presents did Jacob offer to Esau?
7. What did Esau mean to show when he accepted the gifts?

What would you do in their place?
1. Ben ran out of the school building and knocked down Jim. He stopped at once and helped Jim up. Then he excused himself. What would you do if you were in Jim's place?
2. Marie was playing house with her friend Dorine. Dorine took Marie's doll out for a walk and broke her arm. She was

Esau put his arms about his brother's neck and kissed him.

very sorry that it happened. What would you do in Marie's place?

3. Peter had a fight with his chum Dick, and now both are angry with each other. It is Saturday afternoon and the boys are to go to confession on that day. Tell the class what they should do before going to confession. Suppose Peter says it was all Dick's fault, what would you say to him?

4. Mildred has been asked to stay at home on a Sunday afternoon to take care of the baby while her parents go out visiting. Mildred pouts all afternoon and evening and does not treat her little sister kindly. If you were in Mildred's place, what would you do?

5. Jacob told Esau to take of the blessings which the Lord had given to him. Would you have given Esau any gifts if you had been in Jacob's place?

6. On the way home from school Eva runs an errand for Mrs. Hale. When she returns Mrs. Hale gives her four lovely apples. If you were Eva, what would you do with them?

7. On the name day of the parish priest each pupil of the fourth grade gets a stick of candy. Billy saves his to take home and share it with mother and the baby. Do you think Billy is foolish?

8. Violet gets a quarter to spend on her birthday. She has two sisters and two brothers younger than herself. What would you do with the quarter if you were in her place?

9. Charlie's uncle sends him a game for Christmas. Charlie has many games at home which he does not care for. Next door to Charlie's house lives a poor little crippled boy who has no games of his own. What would you suggest Charlie do with the game?

10. Fay's grandmother gives her a large bouquet of flowers from her garden. Tell different ways in which Fay could share her pleasure with others.

70 BEFORE CHRIST CAME

Interesting things for you to do:

1. Jesus forgave his enemies on the cross. Find the words which Jesus spoke to show He forgave them. If you can find a picture of our Lord on the cross, paste it in your character book and write under the picture the words which Jesus spoke.
2. In the *Legend of the Saints* find the story of St. Gualbert and tell it to the class. Dramatize the story.
3. Dramatize the story of Esau and Jacob.
4. Say the Our Father and find the sentence in which we ask God to forgive us just as we are willing to forgive others.
5. If you can find little poems and quotations about forgiveness or about sharing things with others, recite them in class or put them on the bulletin board for others to read.

Good things for you to read:

"Exiled From Home," *Wonder Stories of God's People*, page 15.

"Esau Forgives Jacob," *The Bible Story*, page 46.

Can you answer these questions?

1. When we have offended other people, what should we do?
2. When we have offended God what should we do?
3. How often is God willing to forgive our sins?
4. Why does the priest give us a penance after confession?
5. Can people who die with sins on their souls go to heaven?
6. Where do they go?

20. Joseph, the Dreamer

Jacob had twelve sons. Two of these, Joseph and Benjamin, were the children of Rachel. Jacob loved all his children, but he loved Joseph the best of all. When the boy was about sixteen years old, his father gave him a coat of many colors. His brothers were jealous of him and hated him because they knew that their father loved him better than the rest.

One day Joseph told them that he had a strange dream. "I dreamed," he said, "that we were binding sheaves in the field: and my sheaf arose and stood, and your sheaves, standing around, bowed before mine."

His brothers asked: "Shall you be our king? Or shall we be your subjects?" And they hated him the more for his words.

Another time Joseph dreamed that the sun and the moon and eleven stars worshipped him. When he told his father and his brothers about it, Jacob asked: "Shall I and your mother and your brothers worship you upon the earth?" His brothers became more angry than ever, but his father wondered about the dream.

One day when Joseph's older brothers were out with the sheep, his father said to him: "Your brothers are feeding the sheep in Sichem. I will send you to them."

Joseph answered: "I am ready."

"Go," said his father, "and see if all is well with your brothers, and bring me word about them."

When Joseph's brothers saw him coming from afar,

they said: "Behold, there comes the dreamer. Come, let us kill him and throw him into an old pit. We shall tell our father that a wild beast devoured him. Then we shall see what good his dreams will do him."

But Réuben, the eldest of the brothers, wished to save him and said: "Do not take his life or shed his blood. Let us throw him into this pit."

He said this, however, that he might come back afterwards and return the boy to his father.

When Joseph arrived, they tore off his coat of many colors and threw him into the pit. Afterwards, while they were sitting down to eat, they saw some merchants coming along the road on their way to Egypt. Then Juda, one of the brothers, said. "What good will it do us to kill Joseph? He is our brother. Let us sell him to the merchants instead."

And they took him out of the pit and sold him for twenty pieces of silver. Then they took his coat, dipped it into the blood of a kid which they had killed, and sent the garment home to Jacob, saying: "We have found this coat. See whether it is your son's or not."

The father, seeing the coat, cried aloud: "It is my son's coat. A wild beast has eaten him, a beast has devoured him." And tearing his garments, he mourned for his son a long time and would not be comforted.

Now answer the following questions:
1. How many sons had Jacob?
2. Who was Jacob's favorite son?
3. Why did the brothers hate Joseph?

4. What did Joseph answer when his father sent him into the field?
5. What did Joseph's brothers do to him?
6. Did they all want to kill him?
7. For how much did they sell him?
8. What did the father think happened to Joseph?

Joseph was an obedient boy. When his father sent him to his brothers, he answered at once: "I am ready." That is the kind of obedience that God expects of children toward their parents.

Pick out the sentences you would like to remember and copy them in your character book:

Although Jesus was God, He was obedient to Mary and Joseph.

I must obey my father and mother because they take the place of God.

I must obey cheerfully.

I must obey promptly.

God promised to reward those children who honor and obey their parents.

Father and Mother are my best friends. I will always obey them.

Jesus, make me an obedient child.

Here are some good poems for you to remember:

> My blessed task from day to day
> Is nobly, gladly to obey.
> — *Harriet Kimbal*

> All obedience worth the name
> Must be prompt and ready.
> — *Phoebe Cary*

> If a task is once begun,
> Never leave it till it's done;
> Be the labor great or small,
> Do it well or not at all.
> — *Phoebe Cary*

ROBIN'S DISOBEDIENCE

Once there was a robin,
   Lived outside the door,
Who wanted to go inside
   And hop upon the floor.

"Oh no," said the mother,
   "You must stay with me;
Little birds are safest
   Sitting in a tree."

"I don't care," said Robin,
   And gave his tail a fling,
"I don't think the old folks
   Know quite everything."

Down he flew and kitty seized him,
   Before he'd time to wink,
"Oh, he cried, "I'm sorry,
   But I didn't think."

               — *Phoebe Cary*

More things for you to do:

1. Draw a picture for the poem "Robin's Disobedience."
2. In one of your readers find a story of an obedient child and tell it to the class.
3. Think of Jesus in his home at Nazareth at about your age. Write five sentences telling what Jesus did for his parents to show Himself an obedient child.
4. Give a little play showing children who can obey promptly and cheerfully.
5. Make a play out of the poem "Robin's Disobedience."

Can you answer these questions?

1. Were the dreams that Joseph and the other holy men had the same as our dreams?
2. Do the dreams we have mean anything?
3. Should we believe in dreams? Fortune-tellers?
4. Why must we obey our parents?
5. Whom else must we obey?
6. Have parents any duty toward their children?
7. What are some of the duties they have?

21. Sold as a Slave

The merchants who bought Joseph took him into the land of Egypt where they sold him to Putiphar, a captain in the King's army. The Lord was with Joseph and blessed him in everything he did. Putiphar soon came to like Joseph and gave him charge of his whole household. But the wife of Putiphar was a wicked woman who tried often to lead Joseph into sin.

One day when Joseph was alone, this wicked woman took hold of him and tried again to tempt him to sin. Joseph ran away, leaving his coat in her hands. But she became very angry, and going to her husband with the coat, said: "The servant whom you have brought came to me and tried to lead me into sin; when I cried for help, he left his garment in my hands and fled."

Putiphar believed his wife's words and had Joseph

Joseph was sold for twenty pieces of silver.

thrown into prison. But even in prison Joseph did not lose his trust in God. The Lord was with him as He had always been. The chief keeper treated him very kindly and gave him charge of all the prisoners.

Now answer the following questions:

1. To whom did the merchants sell Joseph?
2. Who tempted Joseph to sin?
3. What did Joseph do when he was tempted?
4. What did Putiphar's wife tell her husband about Joseph?
5. How did Putiphar treat Joseph?
6. How did the prison keeper treat Joseph?

Here are some sentences for you to think about. Try to remember those that will help you most to remain good. Write those that you want to remember into your character book:

I must be clean in thought.

I must never tell anything that is not good.

I must never allow myself to use bad language.

I must never listen to evil talk.

I must use my hands to do only good acts.

I must go with children who think clean thoughts and use clean language.

I must never allow myself to look at evil pictures or objects.

I must never be idle, but keep busy playing, reading, or working, because an idle brain is the devil's workshop.

When others tempt me to do wrong, I must have the courage to say "No!"

God knows and sees everything.

Jesus loves pure hearts.

Mary is the Mother of Purity.

More things for you to do:

1. Three saints are always pictured with a lily; they are St. Joseph, St. Anthony, and St. Aloysius. Can you tell why they hold a lily? Look for a picture of these saints.

2. Learn one or more of the following quotations:

>Beautiful faces are those that show
>Beautiful thoughts that lie below.

It is better to be alone than in bad company. — *George Washington.*

> My strength is as the strength of ten
> Because my heart is pure. — *Tennyson.*

3. Draw or cut out a lily and write under it the words of our Lord: "Blessed are the clean of heart."

4. Read in the *Lives of the Saints* one of the following and tell the story to the class:

St. Joseph	St. Agnes
St. Aloysius	St. Dorothy
St. Casimir	St. Rose of Lima
St. John Berchmans	The Little Flower

5. On a Catholic calendar find different feasts of the Blessed Virgin, and write the name of the feast and the date on which it is celebrated.

6. Learn the little prayer to be said in time of temptation: "O Mary conceived without sin, pray for us who have recourse to thee."

7. Learn the following quotation and say it with the whole class while you point to the American flag in your classroom:

"White for purity, red for valor, blue for justice in the flag of our country, to be cherished by all our hearts, to be upheld by all our hands." — *Charles Sumner.*

If you do not understand the meaning of all the words look for them in the dictionary.

Good things for you to read:

"No," *American Cardinal Reader,* Book IV, page 134.
"Immaculate," *Rosary Reader,* Book IV, page 147.
"St. Agnes," *Misericordia Reader,* Book IV, page 10.
"St. Rose of Lima," *Cathedral Basic Reader,* Book IV, page 40.

Can you answer these questions?
1. How can you keep your heart pure?
2. Can children sin with their eyes?
3. With their ears? Their thoughts?
4. What should you do if someone tempts you to sin?
5. Does God know what you think?
6. How can He know?

22. The Forgotten Prisoner

In the prison of which Joseph had charge, there were two servants of Pharao, the king. The one was chief butler and the other chief baker. One night both servants had a dream. In the morning Joseph saw that they were sad, and asked them the reason. They answered: "We have dreamed a dream and there is no one to explain it to us."

Joseph said to them: "Do you not know that the power to explain dreams belongs to God? Tell me what you have dreamed."

The chief butler told his dream first: "I saw before me a vine on which were three branches. Little by little they sent out buds and after the blossoms brought forth ripe grapes. And the cup of Pharao was in my hand, and I took the grapes and pressed them into the cup which I held, and I gave the cup to Pharao."

Joseph answered: "This is the meaning of the

Joseph told them the meaning of the dreams.

dream: The three branches are three more days, after which Pharao will remember your service and bring you back to your former place. You shall again be his cupbearer as you were before. Only remember me when it shall be well with you and ask Pharao to take me out of this prison."

The chief baker, seeing that Joseph had explained the dream wisely, said: "I also dreamed a dream. I dreamed that I had three baskets upon my head. In the top basket were all kinds of breads made by bakers, and the birds ate out of it."

Joseph answered: "The three baskets are three more days. After that Pharao will have your head cut off and hang you on a cross. And the birds shall tear your flesh."

On the third day was Pharao's birthday, and he made a great feast for his servants. At the banquet he remembered the chief butler and the chief baker. And the butler was called back to take his place once more in the king's service, and the baker was hanged. But the chief butler, when all things went well with him again, forgot all about Joseph in prison.

Now answer the following questions:
1. Why was Joseph in prison?
2. Who was with him in prison?
3. Why were the butler and baker sad?
4. Did Joseph say that he could explain their dreams?
5. Did their dreams come true?

23. Go to Joseph

Two years after Joseph had explained the dreams of the chief butler and the chief baker, Pharao also had a dream. He thought he stood by the river out of which came seven very beautiful and fat cows. Then seven other cows also came out of the river, and they were lean and ugly. And the seven lean cows ate up the seven fat cows.

Pharao awoke. When he went back to sleep again, he

had another dream: Seven ears of corn came up on one stalk. They were full and beautiful. Then seven other ears sprang up, thin and dry, and took away all the beauty of the full ears.

When morning came, Pharao was much afraid, and sent for all the wise men in Egypt to explain the dream. But no one could tell him what it meant. Then at last the chief butler remembered Joseph in prison and told Pharao about him and how the dreams he had explained came true.

The king called for Joseph at once and said to him: "I have dreamed dreams, and there is no one that can tell me their meaning. Now I have heard that you are very wise and can explain dreams."

Joseph answered: "I cannot do anything without God. But with His help I shall try to tell you the meaning of your dream."

When Pharao had told his dream, Joseph said: "God wishes to show you what is going to happen. The seven beautiful cows and the seven full ears are seven years of plenty. And the seven lean and thin cows that came up after them, and the seven thin ears that were dry from the burning wind, are seven years of famine to follow. In the first place there shall come seven years of plenty in the whole land of Egypt, after which shall follow seven years of want and famine."

"Therefore, let the king find a wise and industrious man and make him ruler over the land of Egypt. And during the years of plenty let this man gather into barns the fifth part of all the grain and save it for the seven years of famine that are to follow."

Pharao and all his servants were much pleased with Joseph's explanation and advice. Therefore Pharao said: "Can we find another man so full of the spirit of God? Joseph shall be the ruler over the whole land of Egypt." And he took his ring from his own hand and gave it to Joseph, and he dressed him in a robe of silk and put a chain of gold about his neck. Then Joseph was taken through the city in a chariot and announced as the governor of Egypt, and all the people had to bow before him.

Joseph was thirty years old when he ruled over the land of Egypt. During the seven fruitful years he had the grain bound into sheaves and gathered into barns in every city of Egypt. After seven years of plenty came the time of famine as he had foretold. When the people came to Pharao for food, he said: "Go to Joseph and do all that he shall say to you."

The famine became worse day by day. Then Joseph opened all the barns and sold food not only to the Egyptians but also to the people of other countries.

Now answer the following questions:
 1. How long was Joseph in prison after the chief butler left?
 2. Why did Pharao call for Joseph?
 3. How did Joseph explain Pharao's dream?
 4. What did Pharao do to show Joseph his pleasure and gratitude?
 5. What did Pharao say when people came to him for food?

The dreams of Pharao are explained.

6. Were the people of Egypt the only ones that came to buy food?

God does not forget those who love and serve Him. Joseph's brothers meant to do harm and all the while God was watching over him. They sold him into Egypt because they hated him, but that is just where God wanted him. That is the way God often does with us. He lets something happen to us which we cannot understand, and yet it is for our own good. We must show that we love Him and trust Him. Above all we must never, never give up our hope that He will help us in the end. God sees us all the time and knows what is happening to us. He will never forget us. Only one thing can really do us harm, and that is sin.

Interesting things for you to do:

1. There are many beautiful stories showing how God helped and protected those who trust in Him. Find a story of this kind and dramatize it. The list of "Good Things to Read" will help you find one.

2. Find the poem "The Tempest," by James T. Fields, in one of the readers and tell the story to the class in your own words.

3. Pharao told the starving people to go to Joseph. When we want something from God, we can go to a good friend in heaven and ask him to help us. It is St. Joseph, the foster father of the Redeemer. Find a picture of St. Joseph and paste it in your character book. Write under it the words, "Go to Joseph." Is there a statue or picture of St. Joseph in your church? In your school? See whether you can find one. What does St. Joseph hold in his hand? Why?

4. Look in your geography and find what great river flows through Egypt. What does your book say about the River Nile?

5. Learn a hymn or study a poem in honor of St. Joseph.

Good things for you to read:

"Consider," *The Ideal Catholic Reader*, Book IV, page 182.

"St. Joseph and the Orphans," *The Ideal Catholic Reader*, Book IV, page 193.

"The Writing on the Locket," *American Fourth Reader,* page 64.

"Who Does God's Work," *American Fourth Reader,* page 103.

"The Man of the House," *American Cardinal Readers,* Book IV, page 72.

Can you answer these questions?

1. Who is St. Joseph?
2. Where is St. Joseph now?
3. What is heaven?
4. Do all who die go directly to heaven?
5. Where do they go who die with mortal sin on their souls?
6. Where do they go who die with venial sin on their souls?

24. The Famine Comes to Chanaan

During the seven lean years which followed after the years of plenty, food was scarce not only in Egypt but also in other countries. When the famine reached Chanaan, Jacob sent his ten sons down to Egypt to buy corn. He did not send along Benjamin, his youngest son, for fear that some harm might come to him and he would lose him as he had lost his son Joseph.

When Jacob's sons arrived in Egypt, Joseph knew them at once, but they did not know him. They bowed down low before their brother and he thought at once of the dream that he had had when he was a boy. He spoke to them in another language through an interpreter and treated them as if they were strangers. In a rough voice he asked them: "Where do you come from?"

They answered: "From the land of Chanaan to buy food."

"No, you did not come to buy food," said Joseph. "You came to spy on our land."

But they answered: "We are twelve brothers, sons of a man in the land of Chanaan. The youngest is at home with our father, and the other is not living."

Joseph, however, pretended that he did not believe them, for he wanted to see if they had become better men. Therefore he had them put into prison. On the third day he sent for them and said: "I shall find out whether you are spies or not. One of you will stay here in prison while the others go home with the food and bring back the youngest brother. Then I shall know whether you have told me the truth."

The brothers said to one another: "We deserve to suffer these things, because we have sinned against our brother Joseph." But they did not know that Joseph understood everything they said. And Joseph turned away and wept.

Then he commanded his servants to fill their sacks with wheat and to put each one's money back in his own sack, and to give them provisions for the way. Simeon, however, was kept in Egypt as a prisoner.

When the sons of Jacob arrived in their own home,

they told their father all that had happened to them. Then they poured the corn out of the sacks and each man found his money tied in the mouth of the sack. And they were all surprised and troubled.

But Jacob said: "You have left me without children. Joseph is not living, Simeon is in prison, and now you wish to take Benjamin away also. My son shall not go down to Egypt with you, for if any evil should befall him, it would kill me."

Now answer the following questions:
1. Why did Jacob send his ten sons to Egypt?
2. Why did he not send Benjamin along?
3. Did they know Joseph when they arrived in Egypt?
4. How did Joseph speak to them?
5. Why did Joseph pretend that he did not believe them?
6. What did Joseph command his servants to do for his brothers?
7. Why were they surprised when they arrived home?

25. Back Again to Egypt

Every day the famine in the land of Chanaan became worse. At last when there was no more food left for them, Jacob said to his sons: "Go again and buy us a little food."

But Juda said: "If you will let Benjamin go with us, we shall all set out together. But if you will not let him

BACK AGAIN TO EGYPT

go, there is no use for us to start out, for we shall not be able to get food from the governor of Egypt."

Jacob, however, did not want to let Benjamin go.

Then Juda said: "I myself will take care of the boy, and I will bring him back again to you."

At last Jacob allowed Benjamin to go with them and the brothers went to Egypt together and came again before Joseph to buy food.

When Joseph saw Benjamin, he said to the steward: "Bring the men into the house and prepare a feast; for they shall eat with me at noon."

But the brothers were very much afraid and said: "He brings us into the house on account of the money we found in our sacks." And they told the steward that they had brought the money back with them and more to pay for the corn they would buy.

The steward, however, said: "Do not be afraid. It was God who gave you the treasure in your sacks."

Then he brought Simeon out of prison to them.

When Joseph came into the house, the brothers offered him the presents they had brought for him and bowed down with their faces to the ground.

He greeted them kindly and asked: "Is your old father still living? Is he in good health?" When he saw Benjamin his younger brother, he said: "Is that your youngest brother? God bless you, my son." And he hurried out of the room, for his heart was deeply moved and the tears ran down his cheeks.

Joseph embraced Benjamin and wept.

When he had washed his face, he came back again and said: "Set the table."

The brothers were seated at the table according to their age, the eldest first and the youngest last. And

BACK AGAIN TO EGYPT 91

they wondered at it very much. Then they ate and drank and were merry with Joseph.

Now answer the following questions:
1. Why did Jacob send his sons back again to Egypt?
2. What did Juda promise his father?
3. What did Joseph ask when he saw his brothers?
4. Why did Joseph hurry out of the room when he saw Benjamin?
5. Why were the brothers surprised at the way they were seated at the table?

Do you know what a famine is? During the time of famine people must be very careful about their food and clothing, otherwise they have to suffer very much. Is it ever allowed to be wasteful even when there is no famine? Read over the following sentences and copy those which you would like to remember into your character book.

I must not waste time.
I must save a little money every week.
I must not spend money foolishly.
I must not waste my paper, pencils, or other school materials.
I must not lose my coat, cap, sweater, or other clothing that my parents have to work hard to buy for me.
I must use good judgment by not spending money for things that are not good for me.
I must not waste food.

Famine and plenty both came to us from the hands of God. We should always thank God for our daily bread, and before and after meals raise our hearts to Him in prayer. Never forget to say your prayers before and after meals. When you say these prayers, be sure you think of their meaning and say them with all your heart.

Using good judgment:

1. Edna Keller's mother had promised her a wrist watch for her birthday. A few months before her birthday, her father was laid off and the family had to be careful not to buy things they did not need. Edna did not get her watch and was so disappointed that she cried and sulked all day. If you were in Edna's place, what would you do?

    a) Tell mother that you are glad to help save while father is not working.

    b) Show yourself ugly and spiteful toward both mother and father.

    c) Make believe you don't care whether you ever get a watch or not.

2. Marie Ellson has a good home and gets all the food and clothing that she needs and asks for. When Marie does not like what she is eating, she throws it away. Has she a right to throw away food? What should she do with it?

3. Jim Spalding takes piano lessons from Mrs. Wayne. He is often late, and as Mrs. Wayne has another pupil the next hour, she cannot give him more time. Aunt Nell tells Jim that he is wasting money and also Mrs. Wayne's time, but Jim says she is being paid for full time and his father can afford it. Do you think Jim is right? Has he a right to waste his father's money even if he can afford it?

4. Inez Gray received a dollar for taking care of the neighbor's baby for a week. She spent all her money in the five and ten cent store for little things that she has always wanted, such as a bracelet, perfume, and a ring. Do you think that she used good judgment? What would you have done in her place?

5. Fred Siler went out swimming with his friends. Just when they were starting for home, Fred missed his cap. The boys offered to help him find it, but he said he did not care for it as it was an old cap anyway. Did Fred use good judgment?

6. Dan Meyer is very kind to his classmates. Every day they ask him to let them have some tablet paper. Although Dan is a poor boy, he needs a tablet every few days. Is Dan right in giving paper to everybody? What do you think he ought to do?

a) Say nothing and keep on giving them paper.

b) Tell them that after this they must bring their own paper.

c) Hide his tablet and tell them he has no more paper.

7. Annie Miller's mother always gives her so much luncheon to take to school that Annie cannot eat it all. She wraps up whatever she has left and throws it into the wastebasket. Is she acting wisely? What could Annie do if she were using good judgment?

8. Ed Wade gets a great deal of fun out of marking up people's houses with chalk and breaking down fences. Why is he not showing good judgment?

9. There is an empty factory near your home. Every night the boys get together and have a good time throwing stones into the windowpanes. They say the building is not being used anyway and by and by the windows will all be broken. Therefore there is no harm in what they are doing. Do you agree with them?

10. Two little girls go to the park very often and steal flowers. They say that the flowers do not belong to anyone, and besides, everybody helps to pay for the use of the park. Are they right?

Write the following sayings in your character book:

Look out for the pennies and the dollars will take care of themselves.

Idleness is the mother of want.

Never buy what you don't want because it is cheap. — *Thomas Jefferson.*

Lost time is never found again.

Good things for you to read:

"Hiawatha," The Famine, by H. W. Longfellow.
"The Lost Hour," *The Laidlaw Readers,* Book IV, page 316.

Can you answer these questions?

1. Why may we not damage desks, fences, and other people's property?
2. May we take what does not belong to us?
3. May we keep what we find? What must we do with it?
4. Why is it wrong to waste food or clothing?
5. Who gave us the things we need for life?
6. How can we show ourselves grateful for God's gifts?

26. The Missing Cup

Joseph wanted to make still more sure that his brothers were no longer as jealous and hard-hearted as they had been. Therefore, when the feast was over, he said to the steward: "Fill their sacks with corn, as much as they can hold, and put each one's money back into his sack. Into the sack of the youngest, however, put the price of the corn and also my silver cup." And it was done.

The next morning after they had left the city, Joseph commanded the steward to follow them and when he had overtaken them to say: "Why have you returned evil for good and stolen my lord's cup?"

When the brothers heard why they had been followed, they said: "We brought back the money which we found in our sacks. Why, then, should we steal gold or silver

THE MISSING CUP

out of your lord's house? If you find the silver cup in one of the sacks, let the guilty man die, and the rest of us will be your slaves."

Then each one opened his sack and the steward began his search from the oldest down to the youngest. He found the cup in Benjamin's sack. The brothers tore their garments with sorrow, and returning to the city, they fell down to the ground before Joseph.

Joseph said to them: "Why did you do such a thing?"

Juda answered: "What shall we give as an excuse, my lord? God has found out our wickedness and is punishing us. Behold, we shall all be your slaves."

But Joseph answered: "God forbid that I should punish all of you. He that stole the cup shall be my slave. The rest of you may go back to your father."

Then Juda stepped forward and said: "Let me speak, my lord, and do not be angry with me. When we were here the first time, you asked us: 'Have you a father and a brother?' and we told you about our father and our brother Benjamin, whom he loves so much. And you told us to go back and bring our brother with us. Our father, however, was afraid that some harm might come to the boy, and would not let him go; for he said that it would kill him if Benjamin did not return: Then I promised that I would take care of him myself and bring him home again. Therefore, let me stay instead of the boy and let him return with his brothers, for I cannot go back without him and see my father die of sorrow."

27. The Return of Good for Evil

When Joseph saw how Juda and his brothers pleaded for Benjamin, he could no longer control himself. He sent all the other people out of the room and began to cry so loud that they heard him all through the house.

"I am Joseph," he said. "Is my father still living?"

Then his brothers were very much afraid, for they remembered how they had treated him long ago.

But he said: "Come nearer to me. I am Joseph, your brother, whom you sold into Egypt. Do not be afraid because you sold me into this country. It is not by your act that I came here, but by the will of God, who made me the governor of Egypt. God sent me before you so that you might have food to eat in the time of famine."

"Go now, quickly to my father," continued Joseph, "and tell him that Joseph, his son, lives, and that God has made him lord over the whole land of Egypt. Say to him: 'Come down to me, and do not linger. And you shall live in the land of Gessen and be near me, you and your sons, and your son's sons, your sheep and your herds, and all that you have.' Go now, quickly, and bring back my father to me."

And falling upon the neck of his brother Benjamin, he embraced him and wept, and Benjamin wept also on his neck. And he kissed all his brothers and wept with every one of them. Then at last, they were able to speak to him.

When Pharao and his family heard that Joseph's

THE RETURN OF GOOD FOR EVIL

brothers had come, they were all glad. And Pharao gave Joseph horses and wagons for his brothers, so that they might go quickly to Chanaan and bring back with them all that belonged to them. To each of the brothers he gave two robes; but to Benjamin he gave three hundred pieces of silver and five of the best robes.

And Joseph's brothers went out of Egypt and came into the land of Chanaan to their father Jacob.

Now answer the following questions:
 1. Why did Joseph try his brothers once more?
 2. Who was to be Joseph's slave?
 3. Why did Juda ask to stay in Benjamin's place?
 4. How did the brothers feel when they found that the governor of Egypt was their brother?
 5. Why were they afraid?
 6. What message did Joseph send to his father?
 7. What did Pharao give to the brothers?

Joseph had been ill-treated by his brothers, yet he returned good for evil. He might have put them all into prison or killed them, but instead he gave them corn and put money in their sacks.

When Joseph's brothers heard him tell his dream, many years before, they were jealous of him and hated him. Do you know of any children who are jealous and quarrelsome? Boys and girls who use good judgment when it comes to playing or working with other children and who do not always want to be at the head, are said to show good sportsmanship.

Do you show good sportsmanship?

Check the sentences which tell what you would do if you were playing or working with others.

a) Refuse to play or work along with others unless they do as I want them to.

b) Give other children a chance to choose a game or say what should be done.

c) Play or work along with the others, even if I do not like the way they do it.

d) Stop playing when I lose a game, or stop working because my work did not turn out as well as that of the others.

e) Smile and show what a good loser I can be.

f) Tell the winners they played a good game.

g) Make fun of the other side because they lost and we won.

h) Say the other side came out ahead because they cheated.

i) Quarrel with the rest because I am losing all the time.

j) Not do my best at play or work because I don't care for it or was not chosen to be leader.

k) Do the very best I can, even though I am not the leader or do not care for the game or work.

Do you think Joseph was in any way like Jesus? How many ways can you think of in which they were alike? Look back at the lesson in which Isaac was sacrificed by Abraham if you need any help. There you will find in "Interesting Things for You to Do," how to plan your work.

28. A Father Finds His Long-Lost Son

When the sons of Jacob came home and told him that Joseph, their brother, was still alive, he would not believe them. But when he saw the horses and wagons and everything else that Joseph had sent along, he said: "It is enough for me if Joseph, my son, is still living. I will go and see him before I die."

FATHER FINDS LONG-LOST SON

Joseph fell upon his father's neck and wept.

Then he and his children took all that was theirs and started out for the land of Egypt. On the way Jacob offered sacrifice to God. In the night God spoke to him in a vision and said: "Fear not, go down to Egypt, and I will make a great nation of you there."

When they came near to the land of Gessen, Jacob sent Juda ahead to tell Joseph that he was coming.

Joseph at once took his chariot and went to meet his father. When at last they met, Joseph fell upon his father's neck and wept.

And Jacob said: "Now I shall die with joy, because I have seen your face and know that you are alive."

When Joseph brought his father before the king, Pharao said to him: "The land of Egypt is before you. Find the best place for them and let them live there."

So Israel, as Jacob was called, lived in Egypt in the land of Gessen with his children and their flocks. And the Lord blessed them and multiplied their numbers.

29. Jacob Blesses His Children

Jacob lived in the land of Gessen for seventeen years. When he saw that his life was coming to an end, he sent for his son Joseph and said: "I wish to be buried with my fathers in the land of Chanaan."

Then seeing the two sons of Joseph, Manasses and Ephraim, he adopted them as his own children and blessed them. And calling all his sons together, he gave each one a special blessing.

He told Juda that the Promised Redeemer should come from his family, saying: *"The scepter shall not be taken away from Juda, till He come that is to be sent, and He shall be the expectation of nations."*

When Jacob died, Joseph brought him back to the

JACOB BLESSES HIS CHILDREN

land of Chanaan and buried him there. And all the people of Egypt mourned with Joseph.

Now answer the following questions:

1. What did Jacob do on his way to Egypt?
2. What did God say to him in a vision?
3. Who went ahead to tell Joseph that his father was coming?
4. How did Joseph go to meet him?
5. How long did Jacob live in Gessen?
6. What did he tell Joseph before he died?
7. What were the names of Joseph's two sons?
8. Out of whose family did Jacob say that the Redeemer would come?

Joseph loved and respected his old father. God blessed him for it even in this life.

Make a list of anything you can do to show your love for your parents. Begin with the following sentences: "I can show my love for my parents by obeying them promptly and cheerfully."

Write a play about Joseph and give it before the class. Study the words with which Jacob promised the Redeemer to Juda.

Read the poem "Which Loved Best," and answer the question it asks in the end.

Good things for you to read:

"Helping Mother," *Rosary Fourth Reader,* page 139.
"Jacob Goes to Egypt," *The Bible Story,* page 68.
"Joseph in Egypt," *Wonder Stories of God's People,* page 51.

Can you answer these questions?

1. Who tells us to love and obey our parents?
2. What does God promise to those who honor their parents?
3. Must children always obey their parents?
4. Whom else must children obey?

30. A Man Whom God Loved

At one time there lived a man whose name was Job. He had seven sons and three daughters, and he was also very rich. Job was a simple, honest man who feared God and avoided evil. Because there was none like him on earth, the Lord allowed Satan to test his love by suffering. He wanted to see whether Job would be faithful even when everything went wrong with him.

One day a messenger came to Job and said: "The oxen were plowing and the asses feeding beside them. And the enemy rushed in and took everything away, and killed the servants. I alone escaped to tell you."

While he was speaking another messenger came and said: "Fire came from heaven and struck the sheep and shepherds, and I alone escaped to tell you."

Then a third man came, saying: "An enemy took away the camels, and killed the servants, and I am the only one left to bring the news to you."

And while he was still speaking, there came a fourth servant who said: "While your sons and daughters were eating and drinking in the house of their elder brother, a great wind came and tore down the house and killed all your children. I alone remain to tell you."

Then Job arose, and in his great sorrow tore his garments; and falling down upon the ground and worshipping God, he said: "Naked I came to earth, and naked I shall return. The Lord gave and the Lord has

"As it has pleased the Lord, so be it done."

taken away. As it has pleased the Lord, so be it done. Blessed be the name of the Lord."

When Satan saw that he could not make Job complain against God, he sent him a terrible disease which filled his body with sores from the soles of his feet to the top of his head.

Then his wife said to him: "Do you still continue to trust God? Curse God and die."

But he said: "You have spoken like a foolish woman. If we have taken the good things from the hand of God, why should we not also take the evil things?"

And although Job suffered very much, he did not open his lips to murmur against God.

Job had three friends. When they heard what had happened to him, they came to comfort him. But when they came near, they did not know him, he was so changed by his sufferings. And they tore their garments and wept at sight of him. Then they sat down on the ground with him for seven days and seven nights, but they did not speak to him, for they saw that his grief was very great. At last, when Job began to speak about his sufferings, his friends told him that he was being punished for his sins.

But Job answered: "Although God should kill me, I will trust in Him."

"Have pity on me, have pity on me, at least you, my friends, because the hand of God has touched me." And again he said: "I know that my Redeemer lives, and that on the last day I shall rise again. I shall see God again with my own eyes. This hope is in my breast."

Then the Lord appeared to the three friends and said: "My anger is against you, because you have not spoken what is right to My servant Job. Offer a sacrifice and My servant Job shall pray for you."

A MAN WHOM GOD LOVED

They did as the Lord commanded, and God forgave them because Job prayed for them.

But to Job God gave again as much as he had before, also seven more sons and three daughters. And Job lived one hundred and forty years more in comfort and happiness.

Now answer the following questions:
1. Why did God allow Satan to test Job's love?
2. What did God take away from Job?
3. What did Job say when he heard that he had lost everything?
4. How else did God try Job?
5. What reason did Job's friends give for his great sufferings?
6. How did Job answer them?
7. Was God pleased with the three friends?
8. How did God reward the patience of Job?

What does it mean to be patient? Can you tell how each of the following children can practice patience?

1. Paul is hungry, but mother is looking after the baby and cannot stop to give him anything to eat just now.
2. Mina has a slight toothache. She will have to wait until tomorrow to go to the dentist.
3. Mother wants Jane to go along to the store with grandma. Grandma is old and cannot walk very fast.
4. Albert's little brother is sick and mother asks him to take care of the sick boy while she goes to the store. The baby cries and frets.
5. Bobbie and Teddie are playing ball. Bobbie is only four years old and wants the ball all the time.
6. Can you add other examples in which children can show patience with others?

Write in your character book the sentences which you think will help you most:

I must be patient and kind to old people.
I must bear little aches and pains bravely.
I must not laugh at the mistakes of others.
I must be kind and patient with crippled children.
I must not hurt the feelings of anyone.

Job said: "I know that my Redeemer lives, and that on the last day I shall rise again." In which sentence in the Apostles' Creed do you tell God that you believe that the body will rise again?

* * *

Study one of the quotations:

> Oh, a trouble's a ton, or a trouble's an ounce,
> Or a trouble is what you make it,
> It isn't the fact that you're hurt, that counts,
> But only — how do you take it?
> —*Selected.*

Do unto others as you would have them do unto you.

A little thought and a little kindness are often worth more than a great deal of money — *Ruskin.*

Blessed are the meek, for they shall possess the land.

Good things for you to read:

"One, Two, Three," *Misericordia Reader,* Book IV, page 65.
"How the Children Helped Old Aunty," *Misericordia Reader,* Book IV, page 68.
"The Old Woman of the Roads," *Misericordia Reader,* Book IV, page 77.

UNIT III

Moses, the Great Lawgiver

The children of Jacob were sometimes called Hebrews, which means "from beyond," because Abraham, their forefather, came from beyond the river. They were called Israelites or the Children of Israel, because Israel was the name the angel gave to Jacob. They were also called the Chosen People, because God chose them as the people from whom the promised Redeemer was to come.

Although the Chosen People lived in Egypt for four hundred years, they kept their belief in the One True God and spoke their own language. On that account they were looked upon as strangers.

Since God had chosen the Israelites to be a great nation, He wished to lead them back into the Land of Promise from which Jacob and his sons had come a long, long time ago.

In the following stories we shall learn of the wanderings and hardships of the Israelites, of their ingratitude to the Lord, and of God's great mercy to His Chosen People.

The baby was given the name Moses, meaning "taken from the water."

31. A Princess Finds an Infant Boy

After the death of Joseph the Children of Israel continued to live in Egypt until their numbers grew so large that they filled the land. In the meantime a new king ruled over the country, and he forgot what Joseph had done for Egypt. He saw how the Israelites were increasing and said to his people: "The Israelites are becoming stronger than we. Come, let us make them our slaves, otherwise they will rise up against us." But the more cruelly the Israelites were treated, the larger their numbers grew. Then the king commanded that all the little boys who were born of Hebrew parents should be thrown into the Nile river.

Now it happened that a lovely baby boy was born to one of the Hebrew mothers. For three months she hid him away in her own home, and when she could no longer keep him, she made a little basket of rushes, smeared it with pitch, and in it carefully laid the baby boy. Then she placed the basket among the tall reeds on the bank of the river and told Miriam, her daughter, to watch near by to see what would happen.

Very soon the daughter of the king came down to bathe in the river, and when she saw the basket in the reeds, she sent one of her maids to get it. When she opened the basket, she found in it a crying infant. She felt sorry for the child and said: "This is one of the babes of the Hebrews."

Just then Miriam came forward and asked: "Shall I call a Hebrew woman to nurse the babe?"

She answered: "Go."

And the girl went and called her mother.

When Miriam's mother arrived, the daughter of Pharao said: "Take this child and nurse him for me. I will give you your wages."

The mother gladly took the child and cared for him, and when he had grown up, she brought him to court to Pharao's daughter. The princess adopted him for her son and called him Moses, which means, "Taken Out of the Water."

Now answer the following questions:

1. Why was the king afraid of the Israelites?
2. How did the people of Egypt treat the Children of Israel?
3. What did the king command in order to stop the number of Israelites from growing larger?
4. Why did the Hebrew mother hide her baby?
5. What did she do with him?
6. How long did the mother keep her little boy?

The Hebrew mother loved her little boy very much. She could not bear to throw him into the river. When you were a tiny baby, your mother had to take care of you day and night so that you might grow up well and strong.

Never forget to thank God for giving you a good mother. Love and obey her as He commands you to do. To hurt or disobey your mother would be to displease God, who gave us our good parents to take His place here on earth.

Memorize the following little poem and say it while you look at a picture or statue of Mary, the Mother of Jesus, with her Divine Child in her arms.

THE BLESSED VIRGIN

Mary, the dearest name of all,
 The holiest and the best;
The first low word that Jesus lisped,
 Laid on His Mother's breast.

Mary — our comfort and our hope —
 Oh, may that word be given
To be the last we sigh on earth,
 The first we breathe in heaven.
— *Adelaide A. Procter*

Good things for you to read:

"Mother and Son," *The Ideal Catholic Fourth Reader*, page 90.

"The Mother's Quest," *The Ideal Catholic Fourth Reader*, page 138.

"Our Mothers," *The Catholic Youth*, Book IV, page 285.

"Boys or Jewels," *Misericordia Reader*, Book IV, page 136.

"The Household Fairy," *Misericordia Reader*, Book IV, page 139.

"Moses, the Babe in a Basket," *The Catholic Youth*, Book IV, page 175.

32. Called by God

Although Moses grew up in the court of the king, he did not forget his own people. Often his heart was sad when he saw how the Hebrews were being treated by their Egyptian masters. One day he saw an Egyptian beating one of the Israelites. The man's cruelty made

A voice came from the burning bush, saying: "Moses, Moses."

him so angry, that he struck the Egyptian and killed him.

When Pharao heard what had happened, he wanted to kill Moses. But Moses fled to Madian, where he lived for many years and where he married one of the daughters of Jethro.

One day as Moses was feeding the sheep near Mount Horeb, he saw a bright flame coming out of a bush, and although the bush was on fire, it was not destroyed. When he went nearer to see the strange sight, a voice called to him from the bush saying: "Moses, Moses."

He answered: "Here I am."

And the voice said: "Do not come nearer! Take off your shoes, for the place on which you stand is holy ground. I am the God of your father, the God of Abraham, the God of Isaac, and the God of Jacob."

Moses hid his face, for he dared not look at God.

And the Lord said to him: "I have seen the sufferings of My people in Egypt and I have heard their cries. Therefore I will deliver them out of the hands of the Egyptians. I will send you to Pharao to bring the Children of Israel out of Egypt."

But Moses said to God: "Who am I that I should go to Pharao and bring the Children of Israel out of Egypt? They do not know me and will not believe that You sent me."

And God said to him: "I will be with you. Go and call your people together and tell them that I have seen their great misery and have sent you to bring them out of Egypt into a land that flows with milk and honey, and they shall hear your voice."

But Moses was still afraid that the people would not believe him. Then God said to him: "Throw your rod upon the ground." He threw it down, and it became a serpent. "Now take it by the tail," the Lord commanded. He took hold of it and it was again turned into a rod.

Again God said: "Put your hand into your bosom." Moses did so, and when he looked at his hand, it was white as snow with leprosy. "Now put it back into your bosom," said the Lord. And when he had put it back and taken it out again, it was as clean as the other hand.

"Show these signs to the people," said the Lord. "But if they will not believe even these two signs, take water out of the river and pour it on the dry land. And the water that you will draw out of the river shall be turned into blood."

"Lord," said Moses, "you know that I am slow and uncertain of speech, and since You have spoken to me, I am even slower than before."

And the Lord said: "On your way to Egypt I will send your brother Aaron to meet you. Tell him all I have said. He shall speak for you to the people and you shall show them the signs I have given you."

Then Moses set out for Egypt and on the way he met Aaron, his brother, as the Lord said he would. When they arrived in Egypt, they called the Children of Israel together, and Aaron spoke all the words which the Lord had said to Moses. Then Moses showed them the signs

CALLED BY GOD 115

God had given to him, and the people believed that the Lord would deliver them out of the hands of the Egyptians. And falling down, they adored Him.

Now answer the following questions:

1. Why did Moses feel sorry for the Children of Israel?
2. Why did he leave Egypt?
3. What did he see one day when he was feeding the sheep?
4. Who spoke to him from the bush?
5. Why did the Lord tell Moses to take off his shoes?
6. What did the Lord want Moses to do?
7. Was Moses glad to go at once?
8. What excuses did Moses make?
9. Who was sent to talk for Moses?
10. What did the people do when they heard Moses' and Aaron's message?

God told Moses to take off his shoes because the ground on which he stood was holy.

We use many articles and signs of devotion which are holy. We call such articles and signs sacramentals. Always be careful to treat the sacramentals with respect.

Do you know about the following sacramentals?

The Sign of the Cross:
Do you know what the sign of the cross means?
Do you make it carefully and correctly?
Show the class how to make the sign of the cross correctly.

Holy Water:
When should you use holy water?
Learn the "Prayer before Sleeping." This is an old prayer that people often say when they sprinkle their beds with holy water before they go to bed.

Blessed Candles:

Tell the class when and where blessed candles are used and what is their meaning.

Find in a Catholic Calendar on what day candles are blessed by the Church.

Read "Church Lights," *Rosary Fourth Reader,* page 184.

Blessed Palms:

When are palms blessed?

For what are blessed palms used?

Read and tell the class the story of the first Palm Sunday in *Wonder Stories,* page 268.

Blessed Medals:

Have you a blessed medal?

For what is a blessed medal used?

Find out what pictures and words your medal has on it.

The Stations of the Cross:

What are the stations of the cross?

Can you make the stations of the cross?

During what season of the year do people make the stations most often? Why?

Read the beautiful little story, "Buddy Makes the Stations," *Rosary Fourth Reader,* page 239.

The Rosary of Our Lady:

Can you say the rosary?

What are the mysteries of the rosary?

Which is the month of the Holy Rosary?

On a Catholic calendar find on what day we celebrate the Feast of the Most Holy Rosary.

Blessed Ashes:

When are ashes blessed? What is the meaning of the blessed ashes being put on the forehead?

Study the little poem, "Benediction," *Rosary Fourth Reader,* page 94.

There are many other sacramentals. Can you add others to this list?

Good things for you to read:
"October Stars," *Rosary Fourth Reader*, page 55.
"Holy Water," *Rosary Fourth Reader*, page 87.
"Blessed Candles," *Rosary Fourth Reader*, page 185.
"Immaculate," *Rosary Fourth Reader*, page 147.

Can you answer these questions?
1. What is a sacramental?
2. Name some of the sacramentals used by the Church.
3. What is holy water?

33. Egypt Is Punished with Plagues

After Moses and Aaron had spoken to the people, they went to Pharao and asked him to let the Children of Israel go out of Egypt to offer sacrifice to God. But Pharao refused to let them go and treated the people more cruelly than ever.

Then the Lord sent ten terrible plagues over Egypt.

Moses and Aaron met Pharao at the bank of the river one morning. They told him again that the God of the Hebrews wished to have His people go out of the land of Egypt. But Pharao hardened his heart and would not listen. Therefore, Moses stretched out his rod over the river, and at once the water turned into blood. For seven days the Egyptians could not drink the water of the river, but Pharao would not allow the people to go.

Again Moses came to Pharao and said: "If you will

not let the Israelites go, I will send frogs over the whole land." And Aaron stretched out his hand upon the waters and the frogs came up and covered the land of Egypt.

Then Pharao said: "Pray to the Lord to take away the frogs from me and my people and I will let you go to sacrifice to the Lord."

"I will do as you ask," answered Moses, "so that you will know that there is no one like the Lord God." As soon as the frogs had gone, however, Pharao hardened his heart, and would not let the people go. Then Aaron struck the dust of Egypt with the staff of Moses and at once it turned into clouds of fleas that covered both man and beasts. But the king still refused to let the people depart.

Next God sent a swarm of flies into the houses of Pharao and his servants and over the whole land, and Pharao promised that he would let the people go if the Lord would take away the flies. Moses prayed to God, and there was not a fly left in Egypt. But even now the king would not let the Israelites leave the country.

The Lord sent other plagues upon the people of Egypt, but each time the heart of Pharao was hardened and the Children of Israel had to remain in the land.

At last God said to Moses: "I will send one more plague, worse than all the others, over Pharao and his people. After that he will let you go."

Moses warned the king of the terrible plague that was coming, but he would not listen.

Then Moses called together the Children of Israel and said: "On the day that I will appoint, let each family kill a lamb and roast it at the fire and eat the meat with wild lettuce and bread baked without yeast. And the blood of the lamb shall be put on the doorposts of all the houses in which it is being eaten."

The Israelites did as they were commanded. That night the angel of death passed over the land and entered the homes of the Egyptians, and everywhere he went, the first-born son was killed and the first-born of all the animals also. But where the blood of the lamb was found on the doorposts, the angel of death did not enter.

Then Pharao called Moses and Aaron during the night and said: "Go quickly with your people and sacrifice to the Lord and take with you your sheep and herds. Otherwise we shall all die."

Now answer the following questions:

1. What was the first plague which the Lord sent over Egypt?
2. What was the last plague?
3. Did the Israelites also lose their first-born sons?
4. Why did the angel of death not enter the homes of the Israelites?
5. Why did Pharao let the Children of Israel go at last?

We also must offer sacrifice to God, but we do not offer sheep or oxen. We offer the Holy Sacrifice of the Mass instead, in which Jesus Himself is offered up to God for us. The Church commands us to hear Mass every Sunday and holyday of obligation.

That night the angel of death entered the homes of the Egyptians.

Why did the Church institute holydays? Name the holydays of obligation and place the date after each feast. Use a Catholic calendar if you do not know them all. What does each feast mean?

Jesus is called the Lamb of God because he was sacrificed for our sins. His blood is sprinkled on our souls in the form of grace, through the seven sacraments. A sacrament is an outward sign given us by Christ to bring grace into our souls. The seven sacraments are: baptism, confirmation, Holy Eucharist, penance, extreme unction, holy orders, and matrimony.

Can you answer these questions?

1. Name the seven sacraments.
2. Which of these have you received?
3. Which was the first sacrament you received?
4. Which sacraments does only the bishop confer?
5. Which sacrament should you receive when you are in the state of mortal sin?
6. In which sacrament does Jesus show His great love for us?

34. Walking Through the Red Sea

The Children of Israel were already prepared for their journey, and as soon as Pharao allowed them to go, they started on their way. And the Lord went before them in a pillar of cloud by day and a pillar of fire by night. When they came to the shores of the Red Sea, Pharao again changed his mind and, calling together his army, he followed them in order to bring them back.

When the Israelites saw the Egyptians coming after

them, they were very much frightened. But Moses said to them: "Fear not. You shall see the great wonders which the Lord will do this day: for the Egyptians whom you see now, you shall see no more forever."

And he stretched out his rod over the sea and the water was divided and stood up on either side like a great wall. Then a warm wind blew all night and dried up the ground, so that the Children of Israel could pass through.

The Egyptians rushed in after the Israelites, but Moses again stretched out his hand over the sea, and the waters came together as they had been before and drowned Pharao and all his men and horses.

When the Children of Israel saw what the Lord had done for them, they believed all that Moses had told them. And they thanked God and sang a great hymn of praise to Him, saying:

> Who is like to Thee among the strong, O Lord?
> Glorious in holiness.
> Terrible and praiseworthy,
> Doing wonders?

Now answer the following questions:

1. How did the Lord protect the Children of Israel on the way to the Red Sea?
2. Why did Pharao follow the Israelites to the Red Sea?
3. What did Moses say to his people when he saw that they were afraid?
4. What happened when he stretched his rod over the sea?
5. What did Moses do when the Egyptians followed them into the sea?

WALKING THROUGH THE RED SEA 123

6. How did the Israelites show God that they were thankful for His help?

When the Children of Israel saw the Egyptians coming after them, they were very much frightened and said to Moses: "Why did you bring us out of Egypt to die?" But when they saw the power of God over their enemies, they took courage and walked bravely through the Red Sea.

One of God's great Apostles, St. Paul, said: "I can do all things in Him that strengthens me." He meant that if God stood by him, he could do all things, no matter how difficult. He had the courage to do great things because he knew God was with him.

When we are in the right, God is with us and helps us. We need never be afraid.

Think over the following sentences and copy those that you like best into your character book.

I MUST BE BRAVE

In standing by the right even when I stand alone.
In protecting those weaker than myself.
In fighting against temptation and sin.
By always telling the truth, no matter how hard it may be.
In facing danger that cannot be avoided.
In doing hard and disagreeable things promptly and cheerfully.

Using good judgment:

1. Henry and Dick were playing on top of the garage. Henry dared Dick to jump from the roof down to the paved walk. How could Dick show himself brave?

 a) By jumping down and perhaps breaking his bones?
 b) By saying he will not do it because it is wrong?
 c) By asking Henry to jump first and promising to do it after him?

The water was divided, so that the Israelites could pass.

2. Pearl is out at the lake with a group of girls. They go in swimming and decide to go beyond the danger line. Pearl refuses to go with them because she promised her mother to be careful. The other girls call her a coward and go on without her. Who showed more true courage, Pearl or her friends? Why?

3. Ray's mother is washing. She asks him to take the baby out in the sun for a few hours after school. Ray's friends are coming along the street to play a game of ball. How can Ray show that he has courage?

a) By quickly taking the baby around the back of the house and hiding until they have passed?

b) By going in to ask his mother whether he might go along and leave the baby with her?

c) By explaining to the boys that he is staying at home to help mother today?

4. The boys of St. James school are playing ball out on the street. The ball hits an old man and stuns him for a moment. Which of the following boys showed true courage?

a) Pat says: "Come on, boys, let's go up to him and ask him to excuse us."

b) Bill says: "He has an awful temper, boys. Get out of the way as fast as you can."

c) Ed says: "Just keep on playing and show him you're not afraid. He can't hurt us."

5. May is washing mother's best dishes. When mother is not around she drops a cup and breaks it. What should May do?

a) Put the dishes away and say nothing about it.

b) Tell mother she broke the cup and take her punishment.

c) Tell mother that little brother pulled at the table cover and broke the cup.

6. Elaine is the only Catholic at a party she is attending. It is Friday and meat is being served. How can Elaine show that she is a courageous Catholic?

a) By taking of the meat but not eating it.
b) By eating just a little in order not to hurt her friends.
c) By not taking any meat and explaining, if she is asked, that she is a Catholic.

7. Martin and his chums are walking along the street when they meet a helpless old cripple, trying to cross a busy corner. The boys laugh at him and have a good time watching him trying to get across. What should Martin do to be courageous?
a) Go up to the man and offer to take him across.
b) Tell the boys to stop laughing at him.
c) Pretend he is enjoying it, although he really feels sorry for the man.

8. Bernice is chosen to take part in a pageant. She will need a new dress for the play but she knows that her mother is having a hard time getting enough money together to buy her brother a pair of shoes. What should Bernice do?
a) Tell the teacher she doesn't care to be in plays.
b) Ask her mother to buy her the dress.
c) Tell the teacher she cannot afford the dress.

9. Jim and three other boys are talking about the last baseball game. The boys say that Don played a poor game just because they had not chosen him captain and he wanted his team to lose. Jim knows that isn't true. What should he do?
a) Say nothing at all.
b) Speak up and tell the boys that it isn't true.
c) Go and tell Don what the boys said about him.

More things for you to do:

1. Tell the class as many ways as you can think of in which boys and girls can show courage in little things.

2. Read the life of some saint and tell how he showed courage.

3. Write a little story about a brave act you saw a boy or girl do.

WALKING THROUGH THE RED SEA

4. Fill in the blanks with the correct words: Aaron, song, pillar, Pharao, Red Sea, Moses.

a) .... was the leader of the Children of Israel.
b) God went with His people in a .... of cloud.
c) The Children of Israel walked through the ....
d) .... and his men followed the Israelites.
e) When the people saw how God had protected them they sang a .... of praise.
f) The brother of Moses was ....

5. Memorize one of the following quotations:

"Everyone who does the best he can is a hero."

"He who loses wealth loses much;
He who loses a friend loses more;
But he who loses courage loses all."
— *Cervantes*

6. Find the story of St. Paul, the Apostle, and tell the class how he showed courage.

7. The Church has a beautiful hymn to praise God. It is the "Holy God." Can you sing the hymn?

Good things for you to read:

"St. Ignatius of Antioch," *Wonder Stories*, page 313.
"His Father's Conversion," *Wonder Stories*, page 323.
"The Saint of the Mountains," *Wonder Stories*, page 329.
"Moses Rescues the Jews," *Ideal Catholic Reader*, Book IV, page 140.
"A Day at the Circus," *Ideal Catholic Reader*, Book IV, page 183.
"Each Daily Task," *Ideal Catholic Reader*, Book IV, page 227.
"The Priest Who Gave His Life," *The Catholic Youth*, Book IV, page 278.
"St. Francis and the Wolf," *The Catholic Youth*, Book IV, page 321.

"Two Heroes of Long Ago," *Misericordia Reader,* Book IV, pages 185–207.

"The Twin Martyrs," *American Reader,* Book IV, page 31.

"The Shepherdess Whose Dream Came True," *American Reader,* Book IV, page 42.

Can you answer these questions?

1. Who gave Moses the power to divide the sea?
2. How many persons are there in God?
3. What do we call them?
4. What short prayer can you say in honor of the Holy Trinity?
5. What sacrament makes us soldiers of God?

35. God Sends Food from Heaven

After the Children of Israel had crossed the Red Sea, they came into a desert land. Soon the food became scarce and they began to grumble against Moses and Aaron and said: "Why did you not let us stay in the land of Egypt, where we had plenty to eat? Why have you brought us out into the desert to die of famine?"

And the Lord spoke to Moses, saying: "I have heard the murmuring of the Children of Israel. Say to them: 'In the evening you shall eat flesh, and in the morning you shall have all the bread that you can eat. And you shall know that I am the Lord your God.' "

So it happened that in the evening a great flock of quail came flying into the camp of the Israelites and in the morning the ground was covered with a white covering that looked like frost. When the people saw it, they

GOD SENDS FOOD FROM HEAVEN 129

God fed the Israelites with bread from heaven.

said to one another: "Manhu!" that means, "What is this?" for they did not know what it was.

And Moses said to them: "This is the bread which the Lord has given you to eat."

They called the food manna and it tasted like bread and honey.

Every day for forty years God fed the Children of Israel with this bread from heaven until they came into Chanaan, the Promised Land.

Now answer the following questions:

1. Why did the people of Israel grumble against Moses and Aaron?
2. What did the Lord send them as food?
3. What did the people say when they saw the white food on the ground?
4. How long did God send down manna from heaven?

God sent manna from heaven to feed His children bodily. When Jesus came upon earth, He gave us His own Body and Blood as food for our immortal souls. We call this food the Holy Eucharist. When we go to Holy Communion we receive Jesus Himself into our hearts. How wonderful is the gift which we receive from Jesus in Holy Communion. Much more wonderful than the bread which came from heaven to feed the Children of Israel in the desert. He is food, not only for our bodies, but also for our souls.

Study the poem, "A Child's Wish," by Father A. J. Ryan, and say it for Jesus when you go to church.

Write the poem on a clean sheet of paper or in your character book and make a drawing to match each wish. Next to the first wish you can make a key. What would you make next to the second?

Can you answer these questions?

1. What is the Holy Eucharist?
2. When did Christ give us the Sacrament of the Holy Eucharist?
3. Who changes the bread and wine into the Body and Blood of Christ? How?

4. Who gave the priest this power?
5. When is bread and wine changed into the Body and Blood of Christ?

36. God Gives the Ten Commandments

In the third month after the Children of Israel had left the land of Egypt, they camped near Mount Sinai. Moses went up the mountain and the Lord spoke to him saying: "Let the people prepare themselves for two days and wash their garments. On the third day I will come down upon Mt. Sinai and speak to them."

Moses told the people what the Lord had said, and on the morning of the third day there was thunder and lightning, while a thick cloud covered the mountain. Then a trumpet blew until the sound grew louder and longer, and the people stood at the bottom of the mountain very much afraid.

Then the Lord spoke these words:
1. I am the Lord thy God. Thou shalt not have strange gods before Me.
2. Thou shalt not take the name of the Lord thy God in vain.
3. Remember thou keep holy the Sabbath Day.
4. Honor thy father and thy mother.
5. Thou shalt not kill.
6. Thou shalt not commit adultery.
7. Thou shalt not steal.
8. Thou shalt not bear false witness against thy neighbor.
9. Thou shalt not covet thy neighbor's wife.
10. Thou shalt not covet thy neighbor's goods.

God gave Moses two stone tablets with the commandments on them.

For forty days and forty nights Moses remained on the mountain and spoke with God. And God gave Moses two stone tablets with the Ten Commandments written upon them.

* * *

When the Lord gave the Children of Israel the Commandments, they promised Him that they would keep them faithfully.

The Ten Commandments are God's law also for us and all His people. Those who do not keep God's law commit sin and will be punished, just as Adam and Eve were punished for disobeying the law of God. But in order to keep the commandments, we must first of all know them.

Recite the Ten Commandments. What sins can be committed against each commandment?

37. The Israelites Worship a Golden Calf

When the people saw that Moses remained so long on the mountain, they said to Aaron: "Make us gods, that they may lead us through the desert, for we do not know what has happened to Moses."

And Aaron said to them: "Bring me the golden earrings of your wives and daughters." And the people brought their earrings to Aaron who melted them and made a golden calf for them.

In the morning the people offered sacrifice to the golden calf and then ate and drank, played and danced before it.

Then the Lord said to Moses: "Go down from the mountain, for the people whom you have brought out of the land of Egypt have sinned. They have made a golden calf for themselves and have adored it. Therefore I will destroy them."

But Moses prayed for the hard-hearted people and said: "Lord, remember the promise which You made to Abraham, Isaac, and Israel, that You would multiply their seed as the stars of heaven, and do not be angry with Your people."

The Lord heard the prayer of Moses and spared the sinful Children of Israel.

Moses came down from the mountain carrying the two tablets on which the Lord had written the Ten Commandments. But when he came near the camp and heard the singing and saw the people dancing before the calf, he became very angry and threw the two tablets of stone down at the foot of the mountain and broke them. Then he took the golden calf and burnt it and ground it to powder.

And he said to the people: "You have committed a very great sin, but I will go up to the Lord and ask Him to forgive you." Then he went up the mountain to pray for the Israelites and ask God to have mercy on them. And the people did penance for their sins and listened to the words which God spoke to them through Moses.

Once more God wrote the Ten Commandments on two tablets of stone and told Moses how the people were to worship Him. And they built a great tent of fine linen and bright-colored hangings. This tent was called the Tabernacle. Inside of the Tabernacle they placed

Moses, at sight of the golden calf, became angry.

the Ark of the Covenant. This was a beautiful box made of the finest wood and covered with gold inside and out. Two golden angels spread their wings over the top. It contained the Tables of the Law which God had written for Moses, the rod of Aaron, and also some of the wonderful bread with which God fed the Israelites in the desert. Whenever the people moved on from place to place, they carried the Ark of the Covenant with them.

Now answer the following questions:
1. Why did Moses go up the mountain?
2. How long did he stay?
3. What did the Israelites ask Aaron to do?
4. What did Aaron make for them?
5. Why did Moses come down from the mountain?
6. What did he do when he saw what had happened?
7. Why were the people saved from terrible punishment?

God forgave the sinful Israelites when Moses prayed for them, and they confessed their wrong and did penance. When we are sorry for our sins and confess them to one of God's priests, they are forgiven and the eternal punishment for sin is taken away.

The next time you go to confession thank God for the sacrament of penance and ask Him to help you become more and more faithful to Him by keeping away from mortal sin.

38. Scouting in the Land of Promise

As the Israelites came nearer to the Promised Land, God said to Moses: "Send men to look over the Land of Chanaan, which I will give to the Children of Israel."

Moses picked out twelve men, one from each tribe, and said to them: "Go up to Chanaan and look at the land and tell us whether it is good or bad. Also tell us whether the cities have walls around them, and whether the land bears much fruit or not."

After the twelve men had been gone for forty days, they returned, bringing with them all kinds of fruits and a branch of grapes so large that it took two men to carry it on a stick. And they said to Moses and Aaron: "The land does indeed flow with milk and honey, as you can see from these fruits. But the men are strong and the cities are great and have walls around them."

Now two of the men who had seen Chanaan, Josue and Caleb, said to the people: "We are strong enough to take the land. Let us go up and conquer it."

But the others said: "No, we are not able to take it, for the people there are like giants and we are as grasshoppers against them."

When the Israelites heard what these men said, they were so disappointed that they wept all that night, and murmured against God saying: "Why did we not stay in Egypt? Why cannot we rather die in this desert? Let us appoint a captain and return again to Egypt."

And God hearing the complaints of His people said: "How long will these people murmur against Me? How long will they not believe all the signs I have given them to show that I am with them? I will strike them with a terrible sickness and destroy them."

But Moses again prayed for his ungrateful people

and said: "Forgive the sins of these people, O Lord, and show them Your great mercy as You have shown it to them from the time they left Egypt until now."

And the Lord answered: "I shall forgive them as you ask. But say to them: 'I will do as you have wished. You shall die in the desert and not one of you shall enter the Promised Land except Caleb and Josue. But your children shall see the land which you could not enter.'"

Then the Lord struck dead those men that had deceived the people. And the Israelites were sorry for their sins and said to Moses: "We are ready to go to the place of which the Lord has spoken, for we have sinned."

But Moses told the people that the Lord would not help them now, because they had complained and refused to trust in Him. So the Israelites decided to march forward without Moses or the Ark; but they were defeated and beaten back by the enemy.

Now answer the following questions:

1. How many men did Moses send to the land of Chanaan?
2. What did they bring back with them?
3. What did they tell the Children of Israel about the land?
4. Who were the two men that said the land could be conquered by the Israelites?
5. Why did the Children of Israel weep all night?
6. What did they say?
7. Why did God not strike them with sickness?
8. How were they punished?
9. Why were they defeated by the enemy?
10. How were the men who deceived the people punished by God?

IN THE LAND OF PROMISE 139

Imagine that the twelve men who returned from Chanaan had all told the exact truth. How do you think the story would have turned out?

Tell the story as you imagine it.

Below are some quotations about truthfulness. Think them over, talk about them with your classmates, and copy those that you like best into your character book.

"No man is wise or safe, but he that is honest." — *Scott.*

"He who is honest is noble.
Whatever his fortunes or birth." — *Alice Carr.*

"Speak the truth and bear the blame."

"An honest man is the noblest work of God." — *Pope.*

"A good name is better than riches." — *Proverbs, xxii, 1.*

"Be true to your word, to your work, and to your friends." — *O'Reilly.*

What would you do?

1. Jean, aged seven, and Joe, aged nine, were playing in the dining room and Jean broke a glass pitcher from the table. Mother asks Joe who broke the pitcher and he will not tell. She thinks that he did it and says that she will have his father punish him when he gets home from work. If you were in Jean's place, what would you do? If you were in Joe's place, what would you do?

2. Helen goes to the store for Mrs. Wall to buy two pounds of butter. Mrs. Wall gives her fifty cents and tells her there will be no change. Helen gets five cents change from the grocer. May she keep it without telling Mrs. Wall?

3. Albert does not know how to work his arithmetic problems, and asks you to let him copy yours. Is it honest for you to let him? Do you think it is showing kindness to Albert to let him copy? Does it make any difference to the teacher? How

will Albert gain more: by letting the teacher see that he does not understand his work, or by making believe he knows how to do it?

4. Jane doesn't feel like going to school in the morning. She stays in bed and when mother comes in she holds her head and pretends to be sick, but she does not say anything. Mother keeps Jane home from school. Has Jane been truthful?

5. Bob and his little brother Terry go out to the lake to fish. Bob promises his father he will not go in swimming because the lake is dangerous. Bob goes in swimming but asks Terry not to tell his father. If you were Terry which of the three things would you do?

a) Say nothing about it to anyone.

b) Tell father and have Bob get a whipping.

c) Tell Bob he better tell father that he broke his promise. Would it matter if the boys said nothing to anyone? What results might there be?

6. Ruth has on a new dress. She asks Jennie how she likes it. Jennie does not like it at all. Which do you think is the best answer for Jennie to give?

a) I think it's a wonderful dress.

b) I don't like it at all.

c) I don't think I like it as well as the last dress you got, but as long as you like it nothing else matters.

7. Edith is washing the dishes for Mrs. Shane. They are the very best dishes she has. Mrs. Shane leaves the house for a few hours and Edith calls in the little girl next door and offers her a nickel to wash the dishes. Is Edith being honest? Give a reason for your answer.

8. One day after the noon hour the teacher misses a small purse that was left on her desk. Dave saw Sam in the room all alone. What should he do about it?

a) Tell the pupils Sam took the purse.

b) Tell the teacher alone what he saw.

c) Keep still and think that Sam is the thief.

9. The teacher has just left the room and asked all the boys and girls to be quiet and go on with the work. By and by they all begin to laugh and talk but they get one of the boys to watch at the window to see when the teacher returns. When she comes back she praises the class for being so good. Should the class do anything about it?

10. A bent old lady moves into Birdie's street. Birdie tells her friend that an old witch has moved into the empty house. Her friends tell others until everybody hears about it. Is there any harm in what Birdie said as long as no one hurts the old lady? Imagine you were the old lady; how would you feel? What could the children do to make the old lady happy?

11. Joan is sent to the store to buy a watermelon. It cost twenty cents but she tells her mother it cost thirty cents and keeps the dime. Her mother says: "The next time we buy fruit, we will go to someone else. That grocer charges entirely too much."

Later on before Joan goes to confession she puts the dime into her mother's purse. Is that all she has to do to make good the wrong?

12. Peter likes to read. His mother tells him that he may not get books from the public library since there are enough books in the school library. After that Peter does not get books from the public library but borrows them from the boy next door. When his mother asks him whether he has been getting books from the public library, he says "No." Do you think Peter is honest? Do you think there is any harm in what Peter is doing?

Interesting things for you to do:

1. Make a little play about one or more of the following:
a) A boy finds a purse with ten dollars in it.
b) Someone tells a lie about a poor old man. Later the truth is found out.

c) A little girl tells her mother a lie. That night her conscience bothers her. She tells her mother about it and then asks God to forgive her.

d) A boy has the habit of telling lies. At first people believe him but afterwards they do not trust him even when he tells the truth.

2. Draw or cut out a picture of the fruit which the men brought from Chanaan.

3. Make a poster using one of the quotations about honesty.

4. Find little stories and poems about honesty and tell them to the class or dramatize them.

Good things for you to read:

"Labakan: Or the Untruthful Tailor," *The Catholic Youth,* Book IV, page 249.

"Calumny Defeated," *Catholic National,* Book IV, page 203.

"Honesty Rewarded," *Catholic National,* Book IV, page 122.

"Robert Hall's Pony," *The American Reader,* Book IV, page 171.

"The Spies," *A Child's Garden of Religion Stories,* page 143.

Can you answer these questions?

1. What is the eighth commandment?
2. How do we sin against the eighth commandment?
3. Do we lie with the lips only?
4. What must we do if we harm someone by telling a lie?

39. Water from a Rock

For forty years the Children of Israel wandered about in the desert, and all during that time God fed them and took care of them. At one time there was no water for them to drink and the ungrateful people began again to complain and say: "Why have you made us come out of Egypt into this place where there is no fruit to eat and no water to drink?"

Moses and Aaron went into the tabernacle and prayed: "O Lord God, hear the cry of these people and give them a fountain of water, that they may stop complaining."

Then the Lord spoke to Moses, saying: "Take your rod and call the people together. Speak to the rock before them, and it shall give out water." Moses, therefore, took the rod and called the people together as the Lord had commanded. And when he had lifted up his hand and struck the rock twice with the rod, water came forth and all the people and their cattle drank.

But the Lord said to Moses and Aaron: "Because you did not believe that water would come forth when you struck the rock the first time, you shall not bring these people into the land which I will give them."

Some time afterwards Aaron died and his son Eleazar became high priest in his place.

Now answer the following questions:
1. How did God feed the people of Israel for forty years?
2. Why did they complain again?

Moses struck the rock, and water came forth.

3. What did Moses and Aaron do when they heard the people complain?
4. How did God send water for the Israelites?
5. Did Moses and Aaron believe at once?
6. How many times did Moses have to strike the rock before water came?
7. How were Moses and Aaron punished for doubting the word of God?

How good God was to His people in spite of their murmurs. How much He must have loved them and cared for them. Every day He sent manna to feed them, and no matter how wicked they were, He was always ready to forgive them.

Even Moses and Aaron to whom the Lord spoke so often, doubted that He would send water for them to drink.

We must always trust God and believe all that He wishes us to believe.

Say the Apostles' Creed slowly and carefully to tell God that you are willing to believe all that He teaches. If there is any part that you do not understand, ask your teacher to explain it to you.

40. The Death of a Great Leader

The Children of Israel were now close to the Promised Land, and the forty years of wandering in the desert were nearly over.

As the time came for Moses to leave his people, he called the Israelites together once more and said: "I am now one hundred and twenty years old, and I cannot go with you into the Promised Land, for the Lord has said that I should not pass beyond the Jordan river. But

"The Lord will not leave you ... do not be afraid."

fear not, for the Lord will be with you. Love the Lord your God with your whole heart, with your whole soul, and with your whole strength. And teach your children to do the same."

Then he called Josue whom God had appointed as leader of the people, and said to him: "Take courage. You shall bring these people into the land which the Lord promised to their fathers. The Lord, who is your Leader, will be with you. He will not leave you; therefore, do not be afraid."

And Moses lifted up his hands and blessed the Children of Israel, each tribe with a special blessing.

THE DEATH OF A GREAT LEADER

Then he went up to Mount Nebo and the Lord showed him the Promised Land, saying: "This is the land which I promised to Abraham, Isaac, and Jacob. You have seen it with your eyes, but you shall not pass over it."

Moses died upon the mountain and was buried in the valley of the land of Moab and no man knows where his grave is. The Children of Israel mourned for him for thirty days and then looked upon Josue as their leader, as Moses had commanded them to do.

Can you fill in these blanks?

See how many blanks you can fill in without looking into your book. Then look for the rest of the answers.

1. Three great leaders before the time of Moses were: ...., ..., ...
2. The ark was built by ....
3. The little boy who was hidden by his mother in a basket was ....
4. Abel was killed by his brother ....
5. Joseph was sold into Egypt for .... pieces of silver.
6. Bread and wine were offered by the high priest whose name was ....
7. Because she looked around at the burning city, Lot's wife was turned into a statue of ....
8. God commanded Abraham to sacrifice ....
9. .... sold his birthright to Jacob.
10. Isaac married ...., the sister of Laban.
11. An angel gave Jacob the name of ....
12. Moses died on Mount ....
13. Jacob's sons went to Egypt to buy food because there was a .... in the land.

14. While Moses was on the mountain .... built a golden calf for the people.
15. On Mt. Sinai God gave Moses the .... written on tables of stone.
16. The patient man who would not murmur against God was ....
17. The people of Israel wandered in the desert for .... years.
18. On the sixth day of creation God made ....
19. The names of the wicked cities which were destroyed by fire were .... and ....
20. God fed the Children of Israel with .... for forty years.

UNIT IV

Josue and the Judges

For forty years the Israelites had wandered around in the desert. They had murmured against God and therefore were not allowed to enter the Land of Promise. In the meantime their children grew up and took their places. Now the time had come when they should again take possession of the land which God had given to Abraham and Isaac, and which Jacob had left when he went to live in Egypt.

We shall learn in the following lessons how the Israelites entered at last into the Promised Land and how they overcame their many enemies by the help of great and fearless men called Judges.

On the seventh day the walls of Jericho fell.

41. Back in the Land of Promise

After the death of Moses, Josue prepared to lead the Children of Israel across the river Jordan into the Promised Land. The priests carrying the Ark of the Covenant marched on ahead. As soon as their feet touched the river, the water stood up like a mountain on one side, and on the other flowed to the sea. Then the Israelites walked through the dry river bed while the priests who carried the Ark remained standing in the middle of the river until all had passed through. When the people were safely across and the priests stepped on the other shore, the waters of the river flowed on as before.

Now that the Children of Israel were in the Promised Land, and there was plenty of food for them to eat, no more manna fell from heaven.

The Lord now said to Josue: "I shall give the city of Jericho into your hands. Let your men march around the walls of the city once every day for six days. On the seventh day they shall march around seven times and the priests shall blow the trumpets."

The Israelites did as the Lord commanded. On the seventh day the walls of the city fell and the Israelites rushed in and burned the city and all that was in it.

It took Josue seven years to win back all of the Promised Land. Then he divided the country among the twelve tribes of Israel. The tribe of Joseph received two shares, one for each of his sons, for Jacob had promised this at his death.

Josue ruled the people of Israel for many years. When he was old, he called them together and reminded them of all that the Lord had done for them. He told them to remain true to God and to serve Him alone. And the people promised: "We will serve the Lord our God and we will be obedient to His commandments."

When Josue died, he was one hundred and ten years old.

Now answer the following questions:
1. How did the Children of Israel cross the Jordan?
2. What did the priests carry?
3. Why did the manna no longer fall?
4. How many days did the Israelites march around Jericho?
5. What happened on the seventh day?
6. Into how many parts was Chanaan divided?
7. Why did the tribe of Joseph get two parts?
8. What promise did the Israelites make to Josue?

When the Lord gave the people of Israel the Ten Commandments on Mt. Sinai, they promised that they would serve God and obey His commandments. Now in the land of Chanaan they made the promise once more to Josue.

When you were baptized as a tiny infant, your godparents promised for you that you would be true to God and His Church. We call this promise the baptismal vows. When you grew older, you made these promises yourself. Did you ever renew your baptismal vows? When?

Renew your baptismal vows each year on your birthday by promising God, like the Israelites, that you will always serve Him and keep His commandments.

Interesting things for you to find out:

If you cannot answer all these questions, ask your parents to help you.
1. When were you baptized?
2. Who baptized you?
3. In what church and city were you baptized?
4. Who were your godparents?
5. What did your godparents do for you at baptism?
6. What should godparents do for their godchildren after baptism?
7. On what day is the feast of your patron saint?
8. Tell something about the life of your patron saint.

Can you answer the following questions?
1. When did you become a child of the Catholic Church?
2. What is baptism?
3. What does baptism do for the soul?
4. How often can you receive the sacrament of baptism?
5. Who may baptize? How is baptism given?
6. Why do you receive a name in baptism?

Good things for you to read:

"St. John the Baptist," *Ideal Catholic Reader*, Book IV, page 37.
"Father Brebeuf," *American Reader*, page 192.
"The Life of the Soul," *Rosary Fourth Reader*, page 283.

42. Gedeon, the First of the Judges

While Josue ruled over the Israelites, they adored the One True God. But not long after his death they began to marry the people of Chanaan and to worship idols.

To punish them for their wickedness, God let them fall into the hands of their enemies. But whenever they were sorry for their sins and turned to Him again, He had pity on them and helped them. God chose great and brave leaders, who were called Judges, to help them overcome their enemies. In all there were fourteen Judges who ruled the Israelites for over three hundred years.

For seven years the Children of Israel were much troubled by the Madianites, who destroyed their crops and took away their herds. They cried to the Lord for help against their enemies. Therefore the Lord sent an angel to Gedeon, who was in his field threshing wheat. The angel said to him: "The Lord is with you, brave man! You shall deliver Israel from the hand of the enemy."

Gedeon wanted to make sure that God had called him, and said: "Lord, if You will save Israel by my hand, give me a sign. I will put this fleece of wool on the floor. If dew covers the fleece only, and the ground around it remains dry, then I shall know that I am to deliver Israel."

The next morning the fleece was so wet with dew that the water from it filled a vessel. But Gedeon said again: "Do not be angry with me, Lord, if I ask once more for a sign. I pray, this time let the fleece be dry and all the ground wet with dew." And in the morning the fleece was dry, while all the ground was wet with dew.

GEDEON, FIRST OF THE JUDGES

Then Gedeon called the Children of Israel together to lead them against the enemy. But the Lord said to him: "There are too many people with you. Israel shall not say that they overcame the enemy by their own strength. Tell those who are afraid to return home."

A large number of the men turned back, but still there were ten thousand left. Again the Lord said: "There are still too many men. Watch them as they pass to drink from the river. Those that dip out water with their hands as they pass shall remain; but those that stop and kneel down to drink, shall go back home." Out of all the men that passed, only three hundred were left to fight against the enemy.

Gedeon divided his men into three groups and gave each of them a trumpet and an empty pitcher with a lamp inside. Then he said: "Do whatever I do." At midnight they marched into the camp of the enemy, blew their trumpets and knocked their pitchers together until they broke. When the Madianites heard the great noise and saw all the lights, they became so frightened that many took up their swords and killed one another instead of killing their enemies. Those who remained fled and were driven out of the country by the Israelites.

Gedeon won many other victories over the enemies of his people. While he ruled the Children of Israel, they remained true to God. But after he had died they again forgot the Lord who had delivered them out of the hands of their enemies.

The next morning the fleece was wet with dew.

GEDEON, FIRST OF THE JUDGES

Now answer the following questions:

1. Whom did God call to deliver the Israelites from the hands of the Madianites?
2. What did Gedeon ask of God as a sign?
3. How many men did Gedeon take with him?
4. What did he give to each one?
5. Why were the Madianites so frightened?
6. What happened to those Madianites who were left?
7. Did the Israelites remain true to God after Gedeon's death?

Gedeon was a poor man. He did not expect to be called as a leader of his people. But as soon as he was sure that God wanted him, he went gladly.

God still calls men and women and boys and girls to do great things for Him. He does not care whether they are rich or poor, bright or dull. As long as He is there to help them, they can do all things that He wants them to do.

There are brave men and women who go to foreign countries to win souls for God. They are the missionaries.

You are still too young to be a missionary in heathen lands, but you can be a missionary right where you are.

Are You a Little Missionary?

You can be a missionary:

At home:

By praying for your parents and relatives.

By asking them to go to Mass and the sacraments with you.

By giving a good example to your little sisters and brothers, and telling them about God, the angels, and the saints.

By saving money, stamps, clothing, and other articles for the missions.

By being kind and cheerful.
At school:
By keeping others from doing wrong.
By praying for the missionaries.
By praying for the heathens.
By giving good example to your classmates.
By being kind to everyone.
On the street:
By helping those that are weaker than you.
By being kind to the poor.

Be a missionary: Pick out those practices which you are going to do today.

Interesting things for you to do:

1. Make a mission poster with a picture from a missionary magazine and write the words "Help the missions."

2. If you have at home mission magazines that are not being used, bring them to school and show them to others.

3. Read a mission story and tell the class about it.

4. Make a sand-table project showing a mission in one of the heathen countries.

5. Save pictures about foreign missions and make a mission scrapbook.

6. If your class is not saving stamps and tinfoil for the missions, ask your teacher whether you may put up a box and start collecting.

7. Say a prayer every day for those who do not know God. Perhaps you can get your parents and your little sisters and brothers to join you.

8. Start a mission bank at home, and when you have saved five dollars buy a heathen baby.

9. Read the story "The Young Missionaries," *Ideal Catholic Reader,* Book IV, page 13, and dramatize it.

Good things for you to read:

"St. Patrick," *Misericordia Reader,* Book IV, page 5.
"St. Patrick," *Catholic Youth Reader,* Book IV, page 267.
"A Little Martyr of Japan," *Misericordia Reader,* Book IV, page 18.
"Father Marquette," *Misericordia Reader,* Book IV, page 245.
"A Canoe Trip Down the Mississippi," *American Cardinal Reader,* page 106.
"A Brave Missionary," *Rosary Fourth Reader,* page 247.
"The Protector of the Indians," *Ideal Catholic Reader,* Book IV, page 98.
"Louis, Little Martyr of Japan," *American Fourth Reader,* page 27.
"A Boy's Choice," *Cathedral Basic Reader,* Book IV, page 33.

Can you answer these questions?

1. Why did God create man?
2. Do all men know and love God?
3. Why do missionaries give up their homes and go to heathen lands?
4. What happens to the soul after death?
5. What happens to the body?
6. How long will the body remain in the earth?
7. When will the Last Judgment be?

43. A Faithful Daughter

At one time when the Judges ruled over Israel, there was famine in the land of Chanaan. A woman by the name of Noemi left Bethlehem with her husband and

"Your people shall be my people; and your God shall be my God."

A FAITHFUL DAUGHTER

two sons to live in the land of Moab. After some time Noemi's husband died and her two sons married women from the land of Moab. Ten years later the two sons also died, and Noemi wished to go back to her own country. Orpha and Ruth, the wives of her two sons, started with her on the way. When they had gone some distance, Noemi said: "Go back to your own home, my daughters, for I am old and have nothing to offer you; and may the Lord be good to you as you have been to my sons and me."

Orpha kissed her mother-in-law and went back to Moab. But Ruth would not leave her and said: "Wherever you shall go, I will go; and where you shall live, I also will live. Your people shall be my people, and your God shall also be my God."

So Noemi and Ruth came together to Bethlehem, their former home.

It was the time of the harvest and Ruth went out into the field of a wealthy man to pick up the grain that the reapers had left behind. Now, it happened that the field belonged to Booz, a relative of Noemi's husband. When he saw Ruth gleaning, he asked one of his servants: "Who is this?"

And the servant answered: "She is the woman who came with Noemi from the land of Moab. She has been following the reapers since morning and has not been home for one moment."

Then Booz spoke to Ruth and told her to stay in his

field and at mealtime to sit down with the servants to eat. And he ordered the reapers not to stop her but to let fall more grain for her to gather.

When the harvest was over, Booz called Ruth and said to her: "All the people in the city know that you are a good woman. May the Lord bless you, my daughter." And he asked her to be his wife.

Booz and Ruth had one son, Obed, who was the grandfather of David. *It was of David's family that the Promised Redeemer was born.*

Now answer the following questions:
1. Why did Noemi and her husband leave Bethlehem?
2. Where did they go?
3. Whom did the two sons marry?
4. When did Noemi return to Bethlehem?
5. Why did she tell Ruth and Orpha to go back home?
6. Did they both go back?
7. What work did Ruth do after they got to Bethlehem?
8. Whose wife did she become?
9. Whose grandfather was Obed?

Ruth was not ashamed to work. She was not ashamed to pick up the few sheaves that the reapers had left. She worked hard all day long and was happy to bring home her bundle of grain to Noemi. God blessed her and made her the wife of Booz and the great grandmother of David, from whose family the Redeemer was born.

God loves a cheerful worker. A boy or a girl who tackles every job bravely and cheerfully has the best chance of becoming a good citizen and of doing big things for God and his country.

Can you be honest with yourself?

Check those points that you have been forgetting about and see whether you can be more careful about your work from now on:

I must begin my tasks promptly at school.

I must not waste time while I am doing my work.

As soon as I have finished my work, I must find something useful to do.

When my work is hard, I must not give up, but go on trying.

I must finish what I begin.

I must not be discouraged when I fail, but begin again.

I must not fuss or fret over my work, but do the best I can quietly.

I must always do my homework myself and not ask others to do it for me.

I must not allow myself to be lazy.

I must do my work well and never be satisfied with work half or poorly done.

I must do the work that is given me to do and not choose what I would rather do.

Copy some of the following quotations in your character book:

The harder we have to work for something, the more we enjoy it when we get it.

Be not simply good, be good for something. — *Thoreau.*

Work is healthful. — *H. W. Beecher.*

Work hard; pray hard; play hard. — *Herbert Hoover.*

I believe in hard work and honest sport. — *Theodore Roosevelt.*

When one gets to love work, his life is a happy one. — *Ruskin.*

Do not put off until tomorrow what you can do today.
Whatever is worth doing at all is worth doing well.

Make a list of all the work you can do at home. Then check what you plan to do when you get home tonight.

Using good judgment:

1. Jerry and Edith are home alone on Saturdays. Edith washes the dishes and makes the beds, and Jerry sweeps the floor. Then they are free to do as they please all day. What could the two do to make the time pass pleasantly and usefully?

Jerry sits by the window most of the day and reads adventure stories. Edith plays with her dolls. Do you think they are making good use of their time? Do you think it would be a good idea to plan something else for different hours of the day?

2. The teacher gives the class some problems to work in arithmetic. Frank gets through long before the others. He sits back and waits for the teacher to tell him what to do next. What would you do in Frank's place?

3. Lucille's parents have a drug store. On Sunday mornings when there is very little business, Lucille has to stay in the store for a few hours while her father goes to Mass. She usually stands at the window and watches the people go by. Can you think of something better for Lucille to do?

4. Arthur wants a stamp album. His parents cannot very well spare the money for one just now. If you were in Arthur's place, what would you do?

   a) Try to earn the money yourself.

   b) Wait until your parents can get it for you.

   c) Ask your uncle to get it for you.

5. Agnes takes care of two small children every afternoon during vacation for a dollar a week. One afternoon she wants to go to a show and she asks a friend of hers to take care of

the children without saying anything to the lady she is working for. Has Agnes a right to do that?

6. George is hired to carry bills around to the homes of all the neighbors. When he is about half through, he throws the rest of the bills away. Has he a right to his pay, even if no one knows about it?

7. Harry's father gets him a tool box and some lumber. Harry starts making a dog kennel but gets tired of the work before it is half done. He says he has no dog anyway, so there is no use making the kennel. What do you think about it?

8. Peggy is doing her homework when her friend calls her to come out and play. Peggy tells her mother that the teacher usually forgets to call for the work anyway, so there is no use doing it. Do you think she should leave her homework and go out to play?

9. Charlie's mother has to work very hard to keep up the home since his father is dead. Charlie is ten years old. Is there anything he can do to help? What could a girl do?

10. Nan wants a little kitten for a pet. Mother gets her one, but Nan forgets to take care of the kitten and mother has to do it most of the time. Do you think Nan should be allowed to keep the kitten if she cannot learn to take care of it?

Good things for you to read:

"Ruth and Noemi," *Catholic Youth Reader*, Book IV, page 352.

"Another Kind of Gold," *Catholic Youth Reader*, Book IV, page 370.

"Michelangelo and the Snow Man," *Catholic Youth Reader*, Book IV, page 331.

"The Stone in the Road," *American Cardinal Reader*, Book IV, page 121.

"Perseverance Wins," *Misericordia Reader*, Book IV, page 277.

"Don't Give Up," *Misericordia Reader,* Book IV, page 283.
"Lincoln's School Life," *Misericordia Reader,* Book IV, page 284.
"A Store of Sweets," *Misericordia Reader,* Book IV, page 289.
"Hiawatha's Sailing," *Misericordia Reader,* Book IV, page 301.
"Indian Corn," *Misericordia Reader,* Book IV, page 306.
"The Village Blacksmith," *Misericordia Reader,* Book IV, page 315.
"We Must Wake and Work," *Cathedral Basic Reader,* Book IV, page 225.

Now answer the following questions:

1. What did God do on the seventh day of creation?
2. What commandment tells us to keep the Sabbath Day holy?
3. What does the Church forbid people to do on Sunday?
4. Is all work forbidden on Sunday?
5. Is one never allowed to do hard work on Sunday?

44. The Lord Speaks to a Child

At one time when Heli, the high priest, was judge over Israel, there lived a good woman by the name of Anna. For a long time she prayed that God would send her a son and promised to give him to the service of the temple if the Lord heard her prayer. The Lord gave her a son whom she called Samuel, which means "Asked of God."

When Samuel was still very young, his mother brought him to the high priest Heli and offered him to the service of God in the temple, as she had promised. Samuel was an innocent boy and God loved him very much.

One night while the boy was asleep in the temple, he heard a voice calling him: "Samuel."

At once he ran to Heli and said: "Here I am, for you called me."

But Heli answered: "I did not call. Go back to sleep."

And the voice called Samuel again, and Samuel arose, and went to Heli saying: "Here I am."

But Heli sent him back a second time and told him to go to sleep. The voice called Samuel a third time; and he arose and went to Heli to ask what he wanted. Then Heli understood that it was the Lord calling, and said to Samuel: "Go, and sleep; and if He calls again say: 'Speak, Lord, for your servant hears.'"

So Samuel went to his place and slept. And the voice called again.

Then the Lord told Samuel that He would punish Heli and his sons because although Heli knew that his sons were doing wicked things, he did not punish them. Samuel slept till morning and then opened the doors of the temple, as he did every day. He was afraid to tell Heli what the Lord had told him. But the high priest called him and asked: "What did the Lord say to you? Do not hide it from me."

Samuel told him everything that the Lord had said and Heli answered: "It is the Lord. He will do what is right."

"Say, 'Speak, Lord, for your servant hears.'"

THE LORD SPEAKS TO A CHILD

When Heli had ruled as judge for forty years, the Israelites were beaten in battle by their enemies, the Philistines. The Ark of the Covenant was taken and thirty thousand men were slain, among them the two sons of Heli. When Heli heard that the Ark was in the hands of the enemies, he fell backward from his stool and died.

Samuel now became the Judge of Israel. The Lord was with him and heard his prayers for the sinful people.

When Samuel was old, he appointed his sons as judges over Israel. But they thought more of their own gain than they did of serving the Lord. Therefore the people came to Samuel and said: "Give us a king like other nations have and let him rule us."

Samuel prayed to the Lord to find out His will. And the Lord told him to appoint a king for them as they had asked.

Now answer the following questions:
1. What did Anna call the little boy whom God gave to her?
2. What is the meaning of his name?
3. Why did Anna bring Samuel to the temple?
4. Who was the high priest to whom Anna brought Samuel?
5. What did the Lord tell Samuel?
6. Why were Heli and his sons to be punished?
7. Who became judges after Samuel?
8. Did the people want the sons of Samuel as judges?

Often the voice of God speaks to the heart of man and tells him what is right and what is wrong. Have you ever heard that voice in your heart when you were tempted to do wrong?

Every night before going to bed ask yourself what wrong you have done during the day. Then tell God on your knees that you are sorry.

Interesting things for you to do:

1. Write in your character book "A good conscience is better than riches."
2. Find a little story or poem about conscience and read it to the class.
3. Dramatize the story of little Samuel listening to the voice of God.

Good things for you to read:

"Content and Rich," *Ideal Catholic Reader,* Book IV, page 109.

"A Little Girl and Her Conscience," *Ideal Catholic Reader,* Book IV, page 62.

"Speak, Little Voice," *Ideal Catholic Reader,* Book IV, page 149.

"God Appoints Samuel to Rule Israel," *The Bible Story,* page 108.

Can you answer these questions?

1. When should you examine your conscience?
2. How can we make a good examination of conscience?
3. What should we do before we examine our conscience?

UNIT V
Israel Ruled by Kings

We know that Jacob had twelve sons. Each of these sons became the forefather of a large group of people known as a tribe. There were, therefore, twelve tribes of Israel, and they were named after Jacob's twelve sons.

When the Israelites had taken the land of Chanaan, each tribe was given a share of land in which to live. In place of the tribe of Joseph, however, the tribes of his two sons received each a share, for Jacob had adopted them as his own children before he died. But the tribe of Levi were not given any land because they were priests and had to live among the other tribes.

During the rule of the Judges the different tribes ruled themselves, except when they went out together to meet an enemy. Then they fought under great leaders like Gedeon or Samuel.

By and by the tribes of Israel became so large and strong that they needed a powerful leader to bring them all together as one great nation.

We shall see how the first king of Israel was appointed by God Himself and how the Chosen People were governed sometimes by good and sometimes by very wicked kings.

45. The First King of Israel

One day the Lord said to Samuel: "Tomorrow, about this same hour, I will send to you a man of the land of Benjamin and you shall anoint him ruler of Israel."

The next day a young man by the name of Saul came into the town in which Samuel lived, and the Lord said to the high priest: "Behold the man of whom I have spoken to you. This man shall reign over My people." And Samuel poured oil over Saul's head as a sign that God had chosen him to be king.

When the people of Israel heard that Saul was to be their king and saw how he stood head and shoulders taller than any man, they were very happy and shouted: "God save the king." Then they promised to obey his laws and felt sure that he would help them against their enemies, the Philistines.

For two years Saul led the people to victory over the Philistines, and God was with him in every battle. Then he became proud and disobedient. God wished him to fight against Amalec and to destroy everything that belonged to the enemy. But Saul saved the best of the sheep and of the herds. Then Samuel came to him and said: "Why did you not listen to the voice of the Lord? Why have you done evil?"

Saul answered: "I have listened to the voice of the Lord. But the people kept the best of the flocks to offer as sacrifices to God."

THE FIRST KING OF ISRAEL 173

"God does not want sacrifices," Samuel said, "but wants you to obey. Obedience is better than sacrifices."

"You have refused to keep the word of God, therefore God will have nothing to do with you. He has chosen someone else to be a ruler over Israel." Samuel did not see the king again until the day of his own death, but he wept over Saul for a long time.

Now can you answer these questions?

1. How did Samuel know who was to be king of the Israelites?
2. How did the people feel when they heard that Saul was to be king?
3. What did they say?
4. How long did Saul act as God wished him to?
5. Why was God no longer with Saul later on?
6. What did Samuel say to Saul about obedience?

The Israelites were happy to have a king and promised to keep all the laws that he would make for them.

Are there any kings living today?

Who is at the head of the United States?

The fourth commandment tells us to obey not only our parents but also those who have charge over us. Our parents take the place of God in our homes. The Pope, the bishops, and priests, take His place in the Church. The president, the governors, and all those who help them carry on our government take His place in our country.

God expects us to be not only good children of the family and of our parish, but good citizens as well.

Tell the class different ways in which you can be a good citizen.

Look over the following words and see whether you are a good citizen.

Are you a good citizen?

A good citizen is
- obedient
- honest
- respectful
- clean
- thrifty
- kind
- considerate
- industrious
- polite
- unselfish
- useful
- loyal
- patriotic

Using good judgment:

1. Billy and his friends are in a hurry to cross the street. The traffic signal says: "Stop." Billy says: "There are no cars coming. Let's hurry across." The boys should not cross the street before the signal says "Go" because:
    a) They might be caught by the policeman.
    b) There might be an accident.
    c) A good citizen obeys the traffic laws.

2. Bernice and Martha are in the park looking at the animals. Bernice wants to feed them, but Martha shows her the sign, "Please do not feed the animals." Bernice says she sees no reason why they can't be fed if they are hungry.
    Bernice should not feed the animals because:
    a) The law forbids it.
    b) The keeper might see her and scold her.
    c) Her sister might tell mother on her.

3. There is a banana peel on the sidewalk. Paul sees it and picks it up. He is a good citizen because:
    a) He thinks not only of himself but of other people.
    b) He helps to keep the sidewalk clean.
    c) Somebody might see him and thank him for his thoughtfulness.

4. Ida and her two brothers give a wiener roast out in the woods. When they are ready to go home, Ida throws some water over the ashes to make sure that there is no spark left in the fire. How has Ida been helpful to her country?

5. The children of the fourth grade are having a picnic at the park. All except John are very careful to throw their paper bags and leavings into the can marked "Waste." John says: "There is a man hired to pick up the papers." Who of the children showed themselves good citizens?

6. A man has a fruit stand at the street corner. Someone knocks against the stand by accident and the fruit rolls all over the sidewalk. Ned and Dan have a good laugh about it and help themselves to a few plums. Carl helps the man pick up the fruit and gets nothing for his trouble. How did Carl show himself a good citizen? Should he have expected something for his help? Did the other boys have a right to the fruit they took?

7. Maude goes to the library to get a beautiful picture book about Pilgrims. She likes one picture so well that she decides to tear it out of the book and keeps it for her school project. "Nobody will ever miss it," she thinks, "and my project will be the best in the class." What habits of good citizenship does Maude not have?

8. Len and Harold know that they should not ride on the sidewalk with their bicycles, but they do it just to see the policeman get angry. The boys should show respect to the policeman because:

a) He might catch them some day and punish them.

b) He stands for the law of our country.

c) He might tell their fathers on them.

9. On the fourth of July the American flag is blown down from Tom's house during a terrible storm. Tom runs out during the storm to pick up the flag and is soaked with rain. Walter says Tom was foolish. Lee thinks Tom should have

waited until the storm was over. Tom says that he loves the flag because it stands for all that is good and beautiful in our country and thinks he was right in saving it at once before it could become wet and soiled. Who do you think is right?

10. Catherine asks her older brother Nick to help her clean the back yard which is very disorderly and dirty looking. She says that they were told in school to clean their yards and help make the town look better. Nick says that it is their back yard and it is nobody else's business what they keep in it. Do you think Nick shows good citizenship?

Interesting things for you to do:

1. Write a list of safety rules for your class.
2. Draw or cut out a picture of the American flag and write under it: "I must be true to my God, to my country, and to myself."
3. Give little plays or movies showing how good citizens should act in public places, at school, and at home.
4. Find stories or poems about children who had habits of good citizenship.
5. Write the list of words each of which tell what a good citizen should be and see whether you can find the opposites of the words in your list; obedient — disobedient, etc.
6. Make a list of all the people you must obey.
7. Write in your character book: "Obedience is better than sacrifices."

Good things for you to read:

"To Thee O Country," *Ideal Catholic Reader,* Book IV, page 272.

"Good Citizenship," *Catholic Youth Reader,* Book IV, page 207.

"Barbara Frietchie," *Misericordia Reader,* Book IV, page 236.

"Flags," *Cathedral Basic Reader*, Book IV, page 103.
"A Pioneer Lad," *Cathedral Basic Reader*, Book IV, page 118.

Can you answer the following questions?

1. What promise does God make in the Fourth Commandment?
2. Whom must we obey besides our parents?
3. Is there ever a time when people need not obey those who rule them?

46. A Shepherd Boy Becomes King

The Lord now told Samuel, the high priest, to go to the city of Bethlehem, where he would find the man who was to be king of Israel. Samuel went to the house of Isai and offered sacrifice. After the sacrifice he asked to see the sons of Isai and they were brought before him. When he saw the first son, he said to the Lord: "Is he the one whom I am to anoint?"

But the Lord said: "Do not look to the height or to the face. God sees the heart."

When the seven sons had been brought in, Samuel asked: "Are these all the sons you have?"

Isai answered: "I have a young son who is out with the sheep."

Samuel asked to see him and they brought in a beautiful young boy whose name was David.

Then the Lord said: "Arise and anoint him, for this is the one I have chosen." Samuel took the horn filled with oil and anointed David king of Israel.

David played the harp for Saul.

The spirit of the Lord left Saul and came upon David. Saul became very unhappy and would sit for hours looking sad and gloomy until everybody feared him.

One day when he was again troubled, his servants sent for David, the shepherd boy, to play the harp for him and quiet him with his music. Saul did not know that David had been anointed king, and grew to love him. Saul's son Jonathan also learned to love David very much and the two promised to be true friends as long as they lived.

Now answer the following questions:
 1. Where did Samuel go to offer sacrifice?
 2. What did the Lord say when Samuel thought the first son would be the king?
 3. Where was David when his father sent for him?
 4. Why was David called to the house of Saul?
 5. Did Saul know that David had been anointed king?
 6. Who was the friend of David?

47. David Kills a Giant

The Philistines, the enemies of the Children of Israel, were gathering on a mountain for battle. Just across the valley on another mountain stood the army of the Israelites. Every day there came out from the ranks of the Philistines a giant by the name of Goliath. He had on a coat of mail and wore a helmet of brass upon his head. And he called to the Israelites: "Choose one of your men and let him come out and fight with me. If he kills me, we shall all be your servants. But if I kill him, you shall serve us." And Saul and the Israelites, hearing these words, were very much afraid.

One day David went to the Israelite camp to bring food to his brothers. While he was there, Goliath again came out of his camp and called on the Israelites to fight with him. David went to Saul and said: "I, your servant, will fight against Goliath."

But Saul answered: "You are not able to fight against this Philistine. You are but a boy and he has been a soldier since his youth."

Then David said to Saul: "I kept my father's sheep and there came a lion and a bear and took a ram out of the flock. And I went after them and killed them. The Lord who delivered me out of the paw of the lion and out of the paw of the bear will deliver me out of the hand of Goliath."

And Saul said to David: "Go, and the Lord be with you." And he put his own helmet and coat of mail on David and gave him a sword. But David was not used to armor and took it off again. Then he took the staff which he always carried with him and chose five smooth stones from the brook and put them in his bag. And taking his sling, he went into the valley to meet Goliath.

When the giant saw David, he said: "Am I a dog that you come to me with a staff?"

David answered: "You come to me with sword, and spear, and shield: But I come to you in the name of the Lord." Then he ran to meet Goliath. Putting his hand in his bag, he took out a stone, and shot it with his sling. The stone struck Goliath in the forehead and the giant fell to earth on his face. Then David ran to him, took out his sword and cut off his head. When the Philistines saw Goliath fall, they became afraid and fled. The Israelites followed after them and killed a large number.

Sometime afterward Saul and Jonathan fell in battle, and David became king of Israel. God was with him,

DAVID KILLS A GIANT

David kills Goliath.

for he was a good and holy man. And although at times he committed great sins, he also showed deep sorrow for them. Under his rule Israel became a powerful nation with the city of Jerusalem as its capital.

48. David Sings of the Redeemer

David was not only a good and holy king, but also a great poet. He loved God with all his heart and often poured out his love in beautiful songs. These songs are called psalms. The word "psalm" means a song that was formerly sung to the music of a harp. There are 150 psalms and they are found in that part of the Holy Bible which is called "The Book of Psalms."

Some of the psalms are used to praise God and to thank Him for all His gifts. Others are sung to ask God's forgiveness and mercy. Still others tell us about the promised Redeemer and His Church.

David lived about 1000 years before the Redeemer was born, and yet he tells us many things about Him in the psalms. The following sentences are all taken from the Book of Psalms. You can easily see what they tell about the life and death of the Redeemer.

"He shall come down like rain upon the fleece; and as showers falling gently upon the earth" (Ps. 71).

"Thou art My Son, this day have I begotten Thee" (Ps. 2).

"And all the kings of the earth shall adore Him" (Ps. 71).

"The kings of the earth stood up, and the princes met together, against the Lord, and against His Christ" (Ps. 2).

"And they repaid Me evil for good: and hatred for My love" (Ps. 108).

"And I have been scourged all the day" (Ps. 72).

"I am a worm and no man: . . . the outcast of the people" (Ps. 21).

"They parted My garments amongst them; and upon My vesture they cast lots" (Ps. 21).

DAVID SINGS OF THE REDEEMER

"They have dug My hands and My feet, they have numbered all My bones" (Ps. 21).

"And they gave Me gall for My food, and in My thirst they gave Me vinegar to drink" (Ps. 68).

"And I looked for one that would grieve together with Me, but there was none" (Ps. 68).

"All the ends of the earth shall remember, and shall be converted to the Lord" (Ps. 21).

Because the psalms are so beautiful, the Church still uses them, either as prayers or as hymns. When we say or sing the psalms, we are praising and thanking God in the same words that King David used a thousand years before the Redeemer was born.

Now answer the following questions:
1. Who were the enemies of Israel?
2. How was Goliath dressed?
3. Why did David go to the camp?
4. What did he say when he heard Goliath?
5. Did the king want him to go?
6. How did he kill Goliath?

David loved to sing beautiful songs to the Lord and play them on his harp. He loved also to play for Saul, and it must have made his heart glad when he was able to cheer the king and make him happy again.

Boys and girls should love to sing for God and His Blessed Mother in church, in school, and at home.

They also can find hundreds of little ways to cheer father and mother and other people who may be sick and lonely.

Here are some ways in which children can help to cheer others. See how many more ways you can add to this list.

1. Mother is very tired after her day's work. Bertha says:

"Mother, you rest a while and I'll stay with the baby until he is ready to be put to bed."

2. When father comes home from work in the evening, Jack always has his pipe and his slippers ready for him. Then he runs to get the newspaper and anything else that his father may want.

3. Milly has a little crippled brother who cannot go out to play with other children. She always shares her candy with him and often reads to him or tells him all about school and her friends.

4. Mrs. Gale lives next door to Cora. She is so old that she cannot leave the front porch. Cora often asks her mother to take some flowers to Mrs. Gale. Then she stays a while and talks with the dear old lady.

5. In Tom's class there is a very poor boy who never makes up with the rest. Tom talks to him during recess and lends him an interesting animal book he got from his father.

6. Mollie is giving a birthday party. She invites four poor children who live in the same block. On her note to all who are invited she writes: "Please do not wear good dresses, as we expect to have a jolly time."

7. Mr. Baker lives all alone in a shack. The boys often tease him and make him angry. Eddie and a few older boys send him a pretty valentine with a friendly message.

8. Belle and her big sister go to the hospital every Sunday to sing and play for the sick people.

9. Now add more ways in which you can bring good cheer and sunshine into other people's lives.

More things for you to do:

1. Think of someone whom you are going to cheer today and tomorrow report to the class what you did.

2. Find a little story about a boy or girl who helped to make someone happy, and tell the class about it.

3. Give a little program of songs and poems in honor of Our Lord and His Blessed Mother.

4. Give a play with the following scenes:
Scene I. David comes to his brothers and sees Goliath.
Scene II. David tells Saul that he will fight Goliath.
Scene III. David kills Goliath.

5. Study Psalm 116 which is one of the songs that David wrote. You will find it in *Rosary Reader,* Book III.

Good things for you to read:

"Psalm 99," *Rosary Reader,* Book IV, page 306.
"A Prince of Music," *Rosary Reader,* Book IV, page 292.
"The Giant Killer," *Wonder Stories,* page 110.
"The Shepherd Who Became a King," *The Bible Story,* page 116.

Can you answer the following questions?

1. Why are we on earth?
2. How can we praise God?
3. What hymns of praise do we use in church?
4. What commandment forbids us to use the name of God in vain?
5. How do we sin against the second commandment?

49. A King Who Asked for Wisdom

When David was about to die, he called for his son Solomon and had him anointed king.

Solomon loved the Lord and obeyed His commandments. Therefore the Lord said to him: "Ask for whatever you wish Me to give you."

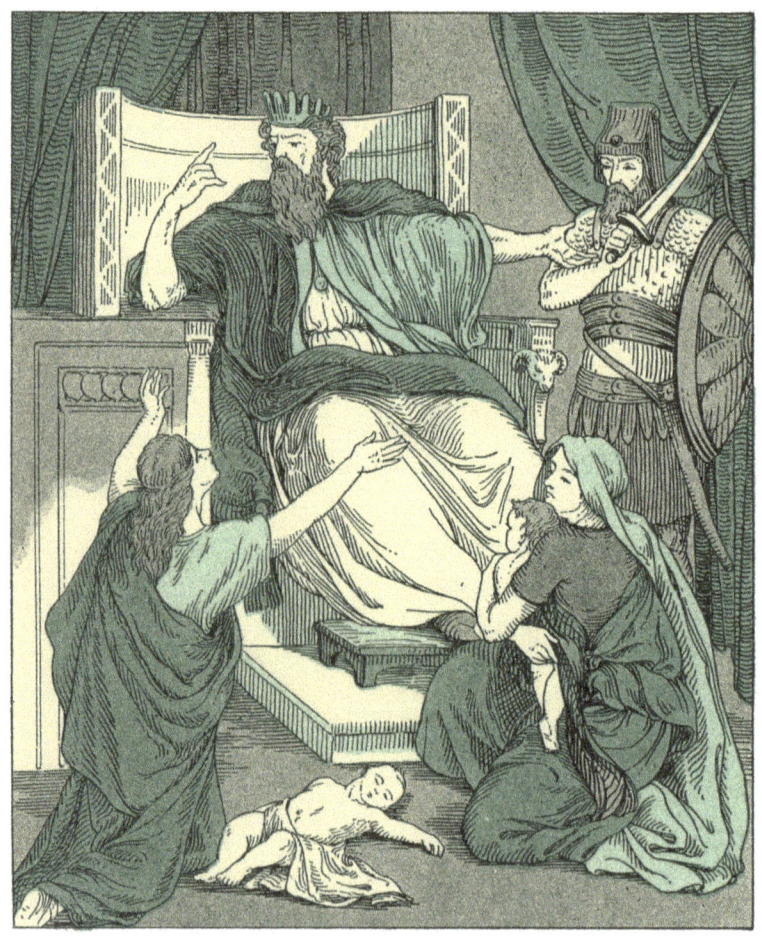

"Divide the child and give each woman half."

And Solomon answered: "Give me, O Lord, an understanding heart, so that I may be able to judge Your people and to tell good from evil."

A KING WHO ASKED FOR WISDOM

The Lord was pleased that Solomon did not ask for a long life or riches or the lives of his enemies. Therefore He said: "I have given you so wise and understanding a heart that there shall be none like you in Israel. And all these things that you did not ask for I shall give you also."

One day when Solomon was in Jerusalem to offer sacrifices, two women came to him. One of them said: "This woman and I lived in the same house, and both of us had a young child. But this woman's child died during the night, for she slept on it. And she took my child from my side while I was asleep and laid her dead child next to me."

"That is not true," said the other woman, "but your child is dead, and mine alive." And so they quarreled before the king.

Then the king said: "Bring me a sword." And when they had brought him a sword, he said: "Divide the living child into two parts and give each woman half."

And the one woman was filled with pity and said: "My Lord, give her the child alive, and do not kill it."

But the other woman said: "Let it be neither mine nor hers, but divide it."

The king then knew to whom the child belonged and said: "Give the living child to this woman, and let it not be killed, for she is the mother."

All Israel heard of the wise judgment the king had made and saw that the wisdom of God was in him.

Solomon ruled over the people of Israel for forty

years. He built a beautiful temple to the Lord and made the country more powerful than ever.

Now answer the following questions:
1. Who became king after David?
2. What did he ask of the Lord?
3. Why did the two women come to Solomon?
4. How did Solomon know to whom the child belonged?
5. How long did Solomon rule over Israel? What great work did he do?

Solomon asked God to make him wise, and God was pleased with his choice.

Often you must choose between right and wrong when there is no one near to tell you what to do. You must try always to choose the right thing to do, no matter how hard it is. In that way you will grow up to be wise men and women. It is such men and women that will be able to do great things for the Church and for their country.

Make a wise choice:
1. Della's mother gives her a dime to buy some luncheon at school. Della buys a bottle of pop and a chocolate bar. Did Della make a wise choice? What would you do if you were Della?
2. Elmer earns a quarter delivering packages. He is a poor boy who never gets any money to spend. That night he goes to the movie to see an exciting show about some bandits who rob a bank. Has Elmer shown wisdom in his choice? What would be your choice, supposing you were very poor?
3. Violet's mother says: "I cannot afford to get you a new dress for your birthday party and a new winter coat, too. You will have to choose one or the other." Violet chooses a new coat. Has she made a wise choice?
4. Billy has a toothache. Mother says: "John will go to the

A KING WHO ASKED FOR WISDOM

dentist with you after school." When the time comes Billy hasn't the courage to go to the dentist and says his tooth doesn't ache any more. Does Billy show himself wise by staying away from the dentist?

5. Millie has to take her medicine three times a day. She doesn't like it and pours it into the sink whenever mother is not looking. If Millie were truly wise, what would she do and why?

6. Sister tells the children in school not to go to the movie that is being shown this week. Mark Roden tells the children it is the best play he has ever seen and there is no reason why they should not go. If the children are wise, to whom will they listen?

7. Rose likes to read many books. The doctor says if she is not more careful of her eyes now, she will not be able to read at all later on. Rose keeps on reading. Is she wise?

8. It is a rainy day but Polly leaves the house without her slicker and rubbers. She says it never bothers her when she gets wet. As long as Polly feels that way about it, should she wear her slicker and rubbers?

9. Frank, Matt, and Joe plan to put electric lights into their playhouse. Joe asks his brother Ed to sneak into the neighbor's garage and steal an electric light. Otherwise they won't let him into their playhouse any more. Ed must make a choice. What should he do?

10. Jack is playing in the basement. He breaks one of his father's tools. If he tells his father about it, he will get a whipping. If he does not, his brother might get the blame, and, besides, his father will not be able to go on with his work when he is ready to do so. Help Jack make a wise choice.

11. The school nurse tells Dot that she must drink more milk and rest after meals. Dot doesn't like milk and does not tell her mother what the nurse said. Is she wise?

12. Mother asks: "What shall we have for dinner today?"

Jerry and Jane answer: "Doughnuts and coffee, mother." But sister Marie says: "Let's have a dinner of meat, vegetables, and salad." Who made the wiser choice?

Here are a few sayings of King Solomon. Copy the one you like best into your character book:

My son, hear the instruction of thy father and forsake not the law of thy mother.

A fool laughs at the instruction of his father.

Fear God and keep His commandments.

Good things for you to read:

"The Little Poor Man," *American Cardinal Reader*, Book IV, page 53.

"Little Wolf's Wooden Shoes," *American Cardinal Reader*, Book IV, page 187.

"Health Jingles," *Rosary Reader*, Book IV, page 137.

"Food," *Rosary Reader*, Book IV, page 134.

"The Story Malchus Told," *Misericordia Reader*, Book IV, page 33.

"Rules of Health Game," *Catholic Youth Reader*, Book IV, page 298.

"The Wisdom of Solomon," *Corona*, page 203.

"The Building of the Temple," *Corona*, page 208.

Now answer the following questions:

1. The fifth commandment forbids us to harm our bodies.
2. What is the fifth commandment?
3. What are the sins against the fifth commandment?

UNIT VI
Great Prophets of Israel

After the time of Solomon the kings of Israel became more and more wicked. The people, too, seemed to forget the Lord and often adored false gods. But God loved His ungrateful children. He sent them great and holy men to lead them back to Him. These men were called prophets.

The prophets often reminded the Israelites of the Redeemer who had been promised to Adam and Eve, to Abraham, Isaac, and Jacob. So far people did not know much about the Promised One except that He would come and save them. Now the prophets told more about Him. One of them told that He would be king, and another, that He would suffer for His people. Their words were very wonderful when we remember that there were still many hundreds of years to pass before the Redeemer would come.

In the following lessons we shall hear about some of the great prophets and learn what they did for God's Chosen People.

50. Elias Is Fed by the Ravens

Achab, the king of Israel, was more wicked than any of the others who had ever ruled over the people. He married a heathen wife and set up an altar to the god Baal whom he served and adored.

One day God sent Elias, a great prophet, to say to him: "As truly as the God of Israel lives, there shall be no more dew or rain until I shall say so." And from that time on there was no more dew or rain in the whole land.

Then God said to Elias: "Go away from here and hide on the other side of the Jordan. There you can drink out of the brook and I have commanded the ravens to bring you food." Elias went to live near the Jordan and twice every day the ravens brought him meat and bread.

In time the brook out of which the prophet drank became dry, because there was no rain in the whole land. Then God told Elias to go to a town called Sarephta where a widow would give him food. When Elias met the widow, he asked for something to eat. She said: "I have no bread, but only a handful of meal in a pot, and a little oil, just enough for my son and me."

But Elias said, "Do not fear. First make me a little cake of the meal you have, and after that make some also for yourself and your son. And your meal and oil will not become less until the day when the Lord will again give rain to the earth." And the widow fed him from that day on, and the food did not become less.

In the third year the Lord said to Elias: "Go and show yourself to King Achab."

Elias went before the king and said: "Let the Israelites and also the 450 prophets of Baal come together on Mount Carmel."

When the people had come together, Elias said to them: "I am the only prophet of the Lord: but there are 450 prophets of Baal. Let the prophets of Baal choose one bullock, cut it to pieces and lay it on an altar, but put no fire under it. I will also take a bullock and put it on another altar with no fire under it. Then the prophets of Baal shall call on their god and I will call on mine. And the god that shall send fire down on the altar is the true God."

All the people agreed. Then the prophets of Baal prepared their altar and called on the name of Baal from morning until noon, saying: "O Baal, hear us." But there was no answer.

At noon Elias said to them: "Call a little louder. Your god might be talking to someone, or he may be away on a journey or asleep." So they called louder than ever, but there was no answer.

Then Elias erected an altar out of twelve stones and made a trench for water all around it. He laid the bullock on the wood of the altar and had water poured over it until the trench around the altar was filled. Then he prayed: "Hear me, O Lord, hear me, that these

Every day the ravens brought bread to Elias.

ELIAS IS FED BY THE RAVENS

people may know You are the true God." At once fire fell and burnt the sacrifice and the wood and the stones and the dust until even the water in the trench was dried up.

When the people saw what had happened, they fell on their faces to the ground and said: "The Lord is God, the Lord is God."

Then the sky became dark with clouds, the wind came, and at last a heavy rain fell. It was the first time in three years that it had rained in Israel.

Elias worked among the people of Israel for many years and showed them God's power and goodness. When his work on earth was coming to an end, he appointed Eliseus to take his place as prophet among the people.

One day when the two prophets were walking and talking together, a fiery chariot drawn by fiery horses came down from heaven and took Elias away from the earth.

Now answer the following questions:

1. What were the men called whom God sent to lead the Israelites back to Him?
2. What wicked king ruled over Israel?
3. Who was sent to the king to tell him there would be no rain in Israel?
4. Where did God tell the prophet to hide?
5. Who fed Elias when he lived near the Jordan?
6. Why did the brook become dry?
7. When did Elias come back to the king?
8. Who fed Elias at Sarephta?

9. How did the prophet prove who was the true God?

How foolish the Israelites were to believe that Baal could hear them. Baal was only a statue that could neither hear nor see. Sometimes children, even Catholic children, believe very foolish things. Read over the following problems and see whether you can answer them correctly.

1. Bert found a four-leaved clover and put it in his shoe to bring good luck. That day Bert's uncle came to visit the family and gave him a storybook. Bert says the four-leaved clover brought him the luck. What do you say?

2. Maggie and Nora had planned a picnic with some friends. After the date was set they found out it would be on Friday the 13th. They quickly changed the date because they believed Friday the 13th to be unlucky. Do you believe it?

3. Frances and Viola are getting ready for a contest in spelling. Frances wears a tiny horseshoe charm around her neck and believes it will help her. Viola prays much for help and studies much. Which girl is doing the better thing?

4. You go to church with a little friend of yours and kneel before the statue of the Little Flower to pray. Your friend says: "That's just what my mother told me. Catholics pray to statues that are nothing but stone. They can't hear or see a thing, and yet Catholics believe they can help them." What would you answer?

Good things for you to read:

"God Watches Over His Prophet," *The Bible Story,* page 118.

Can you answer the following questions?

1. What is meant by idolatry?
2. What commandment forbids idolatry?
3. What other sins do we commit against the first commandment?
4. Do Catholics adore pictures and statues?

5. Do Catholics adore the Blessed Virgin and the saints?
6. How can the saints help us?

51. Eliseus Cures Naaman, the Leper

Eliseus the prophet worked many miracles for the Children of Israel, and they looked upon him as one of God's great men. One day when he was going from Jericho to Bethel, some boys came out of the city and called after him: "Go up, baldhead! Go up, baldhead!" Eliseus looked back and chided them in the name of the Lord. Then two bears came out of the woods and tore forty-two boys to pieces.

In Syria there lived a man by the name of Naaman, who was general of the king's army. This man was very brave and rich, but he was a leper. A little Hebrew girl, who was a servant in the house of Naaman, told his wife about Eliseus, the great prophet of Israel, and said: "I wish my master could go to the great prophet. He would surely heal him of the leprosy."

When Naaman heard about the prophet, he went to tell the king of Syria what the little girl had told his wife. The king said: "Go, and I will send a letter to the king of Israel."

Naaman started at once and brought the letter to the king of Israel. But when the king saw the letter, he tore his garments and said: "Am I a god, that the king of Syria should ask me to cure a sick man? He is only looking for an excuse to make war against me."

"Go, and wash seven times in the Jordan."

When Eliseus heard these things, he sent to the king of Israel, saying: "Why have you torn your garments? Let Naaman come to me and let him know that there is a prophet in Israel."

So Naaman came with his horses and chariots, and

stood at the door of the house of Eliseus. And the prophet sent a messenger to him, saying: "Go, and wash seven times in the Jordan and you shall be healed."

But Naaman was angry and said: "I thought he would come out to me and pray to the Lord and put his hand on me to heal my leprosy. Are not our rivers better than all the waters of Israel? Why cannot I wash in one of them and be healed?" And he turned to go away.

Then his servants said to him: "Father, if the prophet had told you to do something great, surely you would have done it. Why not do the easy thing which the prophet told you to do?"

So Naaman went down and washed in the Jordan seven times as he had been told by the prophet, and he was cured of his leprosy.

And he came back to Eliseus and said: "Now I know there is no other God but the God of Israel." And he offered the prophet rich gifts. But Eliseus would not accept them.

When Naaman was on his way back to Syria, the servant of Eliseus followed him and asked for some of the gifts which the general had offered to the prophet. He made believe that Eliseus wanted the gifts for someone else.

Eliseus, however, knew what his servant was doing, and said to him when he returned: "Because you have done this, the leprosy of Naaman will come upon you and your children forever."

Eliseus died after working and praying for the people

of Israel for over fifty years. Some time after his death, a band of robbers came into the land. A man was just being buried, and when those who carried his body saw the robbers, they threw the dead man into the grave of Eliseus. Hardly had the body touched the bones of Eliseus, when the man came back to life.

Now answer the following questions:

1. What happened while Eliseus went from Jericho to Bethel?
2. Where did Naaman live?
3. How did Naaman know about Eliseus?
4. To whom did the king of Syria send a letter?
5. What did Eliseus tell Naaman to do?
6. How was Naaman healed?
7. Why was the servant of Eliseus punished?

God worked a miracle by the bones of Eliseus, to show how much He thinks of the bodies of His saints. The saints were God's friends on earth, and are now with Him in heaven. We honor God by honoring His friends. Have you ever seen the relic of a saint? Are there any relics in your church?

The servant of Eliseus was punished because he took what did not belong to him. Against what commandment did he sin? See whether you can answer the following questions correctly:

Using good judgment:

1. On the way home from the store Elaine finds a pocketbook with five dollars in it. She keeps it to buy a birthday gift for her mother. Does the money belong to Elaine? If you were in Elaine's place, what would you do?
2. Buddy seldom has any pen or pencil of his own. When he needs one in school he takes it from somebody else's desk. Bill says that's stealing, but Buddy claims he is only borrowing

the things, although he forgets to give them back. What do you think of Buddy's habit?

3. Mrs. Mill sends Eva to town for some ribbon. She says: "It will cost you fifty cents." That day there is a sale and the ribbon costs only forty cents. When Eva gets back she does not return the ten cents. Mrs. Mill gives her ten cents for doing her shopping. Has Eva a right to keep the twenty cents?

4. Every day when Roger comes home he has a pencil, or tablet, or knife that he says he found in school. His big brother says he is a bright boy who keeps his eyes open. His sister doesn't say anything when he shows her the things he finds. If you were a big brother of Roger's what would you do?

5. Whenever Leo passes the grocery store on his way to school, he helps himself to an apple or a carrot or whatever he can get hold of. He says the grocer wouldn't care if he knew because his mother does her buying from him. Do you think Leo has a right to help himself?

6. Nell and Dorothy visit a church. Before one of the statues they find a dollar bill. They take it and go to a show. They both say they found the dollar. Had they a right to keep this? Does it make a difference that they took it from church? What must they do to make up for what they took?

7. Paul steals money from home and treats his friends with candy. Dick knows that Paul steals the money, but he takes candy from Paul. He says Paul does not steal the candy. What would you do? Ought Dick to tell anybody about Paul's stealing?

8. Your teacher asks the boys and girls to bring old magazines and papers to school for a paper sale. You take a bundle of magazines from home without saying anything. Have you a right to give them away?

9. Margaret uses Ann's roller skates during the noon hour. One of the skates breaks and Margaret puts them back without saying anything to Ann. What must Margaret do?

10. Arthur and Matt work all day Saturday for Mr. Roy. He promised them fifty cents each. In the evening he gives Matt $1.50 for both. Matt keeps the dollar and gives Arthur fifty cents without telling him how much he got. Has Matt a right to keep a dollar for himself?

Good things for you to read:

"Paul's Temptation," *Cathedral Basic Reader*, Book IV, page 111.

Can you answer the following questions?

1. What is the first commandment?
2. Does the first commandment forbid us to pray to the saints?
3. Who is the highest among the saints?
4. What is a relic?
5. May a Catholic honor a relic?
6. What does the seventh commandment forbid?
7. May you keep whatever you find?
8. What must you do if you have taken money or other articles that do not belong to you?

52. A Good Father's Teachings

At one time when the Israelites had again become very wicked, God allowed them to be overcome by the Assyrians who took many of the people away to their country as slaves. Among those who were captured was a man named Tobias. This man loved God and kept His commandments.

Every day Tobias went among the poor captive Israelites and helped them wherever he could. He fed the

A GOOD FATHER'S TEACHINGS

hungry, gave clothes to the naked, and buried the bodies of those that had been killed by their cruel masters.

One day when Tobias was very tired from burying the dead, he came to his house where he lay down by the wall and fell asleep. While he was sleeping, some dirt from a swallow's nest fell upon his eyes and made him blind.

Tobias had a young son whom he called by his own name. The boy was brought up to fear God and keep away from all sin.

Thinking that he would soon die, the father called the young Tobias and gave him the following instructions:

When God takes my soul, bury my body.

Honor your mother all the days of her life, for she has suffered much for you.

Keep God in your mind and do not commit sin or break the commandments of the Lord.

Do not turn away your face from the poor and the Lord will not turn away His face from you.

If you have much, give a great deal; if you have little, give willingly even a little.

Keep yourself pure and never allow pride to come into your heart.

If anyone has done work for you, pay him his wages at once.

See that you never do to others what you do not wish others to do to you.

Share your bread with the hungry and poor and cover the naked with garments.

Bless God at all times and ask Him to help and direct you.

Do not fear, my son. We lead a poor life, but if we fear God and do good, we shall have many things.

Now answer the following questions:
1. Why did God let the Assyrians capture the Israelites?
2. Who was the man that fed the hungry and buried the dead?
3. What happened to this holy man one day when he was asleep?
4. How was young Tobias brought up?
5. What advice did Tobias give his young son about his mother?

Tobias loved and served those around him.

We should love our neighbor because God loves him, and because we are all children of the same Father in heaven. Everybody is our neighbor.

We show our love for our neighbor by helping him whenever he is in need. The help we give to our neighbor may be either for his body or for his soul. We call the different kinds of help for the body the Corporal Works of Mercy, and those for the soul the Spiritual Works of Mercy. The following are the Corporal Works of Mercy:
1. To feed the hungry.
2. To give drink to the thirsty.
3. To clothe the naked.
4. To give shelter to the homeless.
5. To visit the imprisoned.
6. To visit the sick.
7. To bury the dead.

While you are young and still going to school, your best chance to do acts of kindness to your neighbor is among the children around you.

Interesting things for you to do:
1. Look over the Corporal Works of Mercy and see which of them you can do.

2. Pick out the work of mercy you are going to do today. Perhaps if you read the Corporal Works of Mercy to your parents, they will help you pick out one which you can do. Tomorrow tell the class about the act of kindness you did or which you have seen others do.

3. Ask your teacher to read the Spiritual Works of Mercy to you and see which of them can be done by children of your age.

4. Read once more the advice Tobias gave to his son, and pick out the sentence you would like to remember. Copy the sentence into your character book.

5. Make a list of all the acts of kindness children can do for others.

6. Find in the stories you have already read in this book, acts of kindness done by others for their neighbor.

Good things for you to read:

"The Good Samaritan," *Cathedral Basic Reader,* Book IV, page 30.

"The Miraculous Pitcher," *Cathedral Basic Reader,* Book IV, page 177.

Can you answer the following questions?

1. Who is our neighbor?
2. Why should we love our neighbor?
3. How can we show that we love our neighbor?

53. On a Journey with an Angel

Tobias had once been a rich man. In those days he lent a sum of money to Gabelus, one of his friends, who gave him a written promise to pay back what he owed. Now Tobias told his son to go to the city of Rages, where Gabelus lived, and ask for the money. But the young Tobias did not know the way to Rages nor the man who owed the money. Therefore his father said: "Go and look for a faithful man who will go along with you, and I will pay him his hire."

Tobias went out and found a beautiful young man standing ready for a journey. "Where are you from?" asked Tobias.

The young man answered: "Of the Children of Israel."

"Do you know the way to Rages?" asked Tobias.

"I know the way," answered the young man, "and have often been in the house of Gabelus."

Tobias took the stranger to his father, who asked: "Can you take my son to Gabelus at Rages? I will pay you when you return."

The young man answered: "I will take him there and bring him back again to you."

The father said: "May you have a good journey. God be with you, and His angel accompany you."

The two young men started out together and young Tobias' dog followed them. On the first night they stopped at the river Tigris. Here Tobias went out to wash his feet, when a big fish came up to devour him. Tobias cried out for help, and his guide said: "Take him and pull him out." When he had done so, his companion said: "Keep the gall of the fish for medicine. It is good for anointing the eyes and curing blindness."

They continued their journey until they came to the

house of a man named Raguel. Here the guide said to Tobias: "This man has a daughter whose name is Sara. Ask her father to give her to you as wife."

And they went into the house and were received with joy. Raguel asked them whether they knew Tobias. When Tobias told Raguel who he was, he kissed the young boy and said: "A blessing be on you, my boy, for you are the son of a good and holy man."

But before they sat down to eat, Tobias asked Raguel to give him Sara as his wife. Raguel took the right hand of his daughter and put it into the right hand of Tobias, saying: "The God of Abraham and the God of Isaac and the God of Jacob be with you, and may He join you together and bless you."

Then they made a big feast and Raguel asked Tobias to stay with him for two weeks. In the meantime Tobias asked his guide to go to Gabelus, because he knew that his parents would be waiting for his return. The guide went at once and came back to Tobias with the money. He also brought Gabelus with him to the wedding feast.

At home the parents of Tobias began to fear that something had happened to their son. Every day his mother would go to the top of a hill, where she might see him coming from afar off. At last she saw the two young men coming and the dog running on ahead as if to bring the good news; and she ran to her husband and said: "Behold, your son is coming."

On the way the faithful companion of Tobias said to him: "As soon as you come into the house, adore the

"May you have a good journey. God be with you."

Lord your God and give Him thanks. Then go to your father and kiss him and anoint his eyes with the fish gall which you brought with you." Tobias did as he was told, and when he had anointed his father's eyes they were healed.

Then the young Tobias told his parents all that God had done for him through the help of his faithful guide. And they asked the young man to accept half of all the things they had brought. But the young man answered: "I will tell you the truth. When you prayed with tears and buried the dead at night, I offered your prayer to the Lord. I am the angel Raphael, one of the seven who stand before the Lord." And when they heard these things they fell upon the ground on their faces.

But the angel said: "Peace be to you. Do not fear. Bless God and sing praises to Him." And they saw him no more.

For three hours they prayed upon their faces and blessed God. When they arose, they told all the people the wonderful things God had done for them.

Now answer the following questions:
1. To whom did Tobias lend money?
2. What did he tell young Tobias to do?
3. Who went along with Tobias?
4. Where did they stop the first night?
5. What happened while Tobias was washing his feet?
6. At whose house did they stop?
7. Who became the wife of Tobias?
8. Who got the money from Gabelus?
9. Where did Gabelus live?

10. What did the young Tobias do when he arrived home?
11. Who was the companion of Tobias?

Every one of us has an angel to watch over him. We do not see our Guardian Angel in the same way as Tobias saw Raphael, but we know that he is always at our side. If we could see the angel at our side, how good we should always be to please him.

When we are tempted to do wrong, we should remember that God and our Guardian Angel see us.

Interesting things for you to do:

1. Sing a hymn to the Guardian Angel.
2. Make an angel poster.
3. Find all the stories in this book, which you have read so far, in which God sent an angel to earth.
4. Find some pictures of angels and make living pictures like them.
5. Learn a little poem about the Guardian Angel and recite it before the class.
6. Dramatize the story of Tobias and the Angel.
7. Write five sentences about the Guardian Angel.
8. Find a picture of an angel and paste it in your character book. Under it write the following poem to the Guardian Angel:

> Dear Angel; ever at my side,
>   How loving must thou be,
> To leave thy home in heaven to guide
>   A little child like me.
>   — *Father Faber.*

Good things for you to read:

"What Have I," *Ideal Reader*, Book IV, page 51.
"Guardian Angel," *Ideal Reader*, Book IV, page 52.
"The Children and the Angels," *Ideal Reader*, Book IV, page 103.

Can you answer the following questions?
1. What are the angels?
2. Where are the angels?
3. What do the angels do for us?
4. Did all the angels that God made remain good?
5. What are those angels called that disobeyed God?

54. A Prophet Tells of the Redeemer

The greatest of all the prophets was Isaias. For fifty years this holy man preached to the people and tried to make them repent of their sins and return to God. He told them of the terrible punishment the Lord would send them, but they would not listen. They not only kept on in their sinful ways, but even persecuted the great prophet himself, for telling them the truth.

Although it was still over seven hundred years before the time of the Redeemer, Isaias foretold many things about Him. He told the people that the Redeemer would be born of a virgin: *"Behold, a virgin shall conceive and bear a son and His name shall be called Emmanuel."*

It was he, too, who said that the Promised One would be a king, and that He would come from the house of David. *"A child is born to us, and a son is given to us, and the government is upon His shoulder: and His name shall be called, Wonderful, Counselor, God the Mighty, the Father of the world to come, the Prince of Peace. . . . He shall sit upon the throne of David."*

He spoke also of our Lord's sufferings in these

Isaias preached to the people, and told of the Redeemer to come.

words: *"He was offered because it was His own will, and He opened not His mouth."*

And of the resurrection he says: *"His sepulcher shall be glorious."*

It was this great prophet also who first used the beautiful words "Lamb of God" which we hear every day at Mass and which we use so often in our prayers.

55. Jeremias Weeps Over Jerusalem

After the time of Isaias God sent still another great prophet, Jeremias by name, to warn His Chosen People and bring them back to Him. But the people and their kings had become more wicked than ever before. The more Jeremias tried to tell them of God and His mercy and of the punishment which was waiting for them, the more angry they became with him. At last, with a heart full of sorrow for his country and his people, the prophet said: "For twenty-three years I warned you day and night to do penance, and you would not hear me. Therefore the Lord will send the King of Babylon into this land and the people shall serve him for seventy years." But even then they would not do penance.

Then Nabuchodonosor, the King of Babylon, came into the land and took away the Chosen People to be his slaves. He burned the beautiful temple which King Solomon had built and of which the Jews were so proud, and took away with him all the gold and silver vessels of the temple. The great city of Jerusalem, called the Holy City, was also destroyed. Only a few poor people were left behind, among them Jeremias, the prophet. Sadly he looked over the ruins of the city and wept, saying: "O all you that pass by the way, attend and see, if there be any sorrow like to my sorrow."

Now answer the following questions:
1. What two great prophets did God send among His people?
2. What did the prophets do for the people?

3. What did Isaias tell about the Redeemer?
4. Who took the people to Babylon as slaves?
5. How long did Jeremias say they would stay there?
6. Who was left behind after the captives were taken away?

How many of the following questions can you answer about the Redeemer?

1. When was the Redeemer promised for the first time?
2. Why did God promise a Redeemer to Adam and Eve?
3. List the names of the great leaders of Israel to whom God promised the Redeemer.
4. What prophet said that the Redeemer would come from the family of David?
5. Who was the great grandmother of David?

Interesting things for you to do:

1. Make a list of all the prophets you have read about and write a sentence about each.
2. On the map find the cities of Jerusalem and Bethlehem.
3. Tell the class the story of God's promise of a Redeemer.
4. Read over the story of Job and find what he said about the Redeemer.
5. See how many of God's promises of a Redeemer you can say by heart.

UNIT VII

The Babylonian Captivity

The prophets, as we have seen, could look far into the future. From them the Jews learned much about the promised Redeemer. Isaias told them about His birth, His name, and His death. Another prophet, Micheas, pointed out the city where He would be born, in the following beautiful words: *"And thou, Bethlehem Ephrata, art a little one among the thousands of Juda: out of thee shall He come forth unto me that is to be the ruler in Israel"* (Micheas v. 2).

But the time of the Redeemer had not yet come. God punished the Jews for their wickedness and gave them into the hands of the Babylonians.

We shall now see how the Babylonian kings treated the Israelites and how God still loved and comforted His sinful people.

Ezechiel reminded the people of God's mercy.

56. A Captive Prophet

When Nabuchodonosor took the people of Israel away to Babylon, one of the prophets, whose name was Ezechiel, was brought along as a captive. Although the Israelites were treated kindly by the king, they often thought of their own land and the beautiful temple in Jerusalem. They would sit by the side of the river at night and weep at the thought of their wasted country. In order to keep alive in them the hope of some day going back to their own land, Ezechiel reminded the people of the mercy of God, for although they often offended Him, He had pity on their captivity.

One day in a vision God showed Ezechiel a big field which was filled up with the dried bones of men. He said: "Speak to these bones that they may live again."

Ezechiel did so; and as he spoke, there was a noise, and the bones came together and were covered with flesh and skin. And they lived and stood upon their feet, and formed a great army.

Then the Lord told him that in the same way He would give new life to his children and would lead them back into the land of Israel. "I will open your graves, O My people," said the Lord, "and will bring you into the land of Israel. Behold, I Myself will seek My sheep and will visit them. I will feed them in the most fruitful pastures. I will save My flock and I will put one shepherd over them, and he shall feed them, and he shall be their shepherd. And they shall know that I, the Lord their God, am with them and that they are My people."

God meant to show the people of Israel not only that they would once more get back into their own country, but also that they would some day rise from their graves.

Now answer the following questions:

1. In what land were the people of Israel captives?
2. What prophet was with them?
3. How were they treated by the king?
4. How did God show that He would bring the Israelites back again to their country?
5. What else did the Lord say He would do for His people?

There is one sentence in the Apostles' Creed in which we tell God that we believe that our bodies will rise again on the last day. Say the Apostles' Creed and find the sentence. In this lesson God calls Himself a shepherd, and His people the sheep. Do you know a story that Jesus told about a lost sheep? Tell it to the class.

Good things for you to read:

"The Good Shepherd," *American Reader*, Book IV, page 7.
"Song of Spring," *American Reader*, Book IV, page 278.

Can you answer the following questions?

1. Where does the soul go when a person dies?
2. Where does the body go?
3. Will the body always stay in the ground?
4. On what day will our bodies rise again?
5. What will happen on that day?
6. What can you do to save your soul?
7. In what prayer do we tell God what we believe?

57. Daniel in the Den of Lions

Among the captive Israelites in Babylon there were many young men of noble families. The king commanded that these should be trained for his special service. One of the young men was Daniel. He was very wise and had often proved to the king that his God was the only true God. Therefore he was made governor of Babylon.

Some years later another king ruled over Babylon. He also honored Daniel and made him one of the princes over the governors of the kingdom. But the other princes and the governors were jealous and tried to find some way to destroy him. At last they told the king that by praying to his own God, Daniel was disobeying the law of the country and that he must therefore be thrown into the den of the lions.

The king was very much grieved and tried to save Daniel. But the men hated him and demanded that he be punished according to the law. They even threatened the king and said that they would destroy him and his whole house, if he did not do as they asked.

At last the king commanded that Daniel be thrown into the lions' den. He still hoped, however, that Daniel would be saved. Therefore he said: "Your God, whom you have always served, will deliver you."

So Daniel was thrown into the den; but although the lions were fierce and hungry, they did not harm him.

Daniel was thrown into the den, but the lions did not harm him.

For six days Daniel was left in the den without anything to eat.

Now there lived far away from Babylon a prophet by the name of Habacuc. One day as he was carrying food to the reapers in the field, an angel of the Lord came and told him to bring the food to Daniel in Babylon. Habacuc said he did not know the way to Babylon nor where to find the lions' den.

Then the angel took him by the hair of his head and carried him with great speed to Daniel. And when he had given the food to Daniel, the angel carried him back again.

On the seventh day the king went to the lions' den to mourn for Daniel. He called down into the den: "Daniel, servant of the living God, has your God been able to deliver you from the lions?"

And Daniel, answering the king, said: "O King, my God has sent His angel to close the mouths of the lions and they have not hurt me."

Then the king was very glad and cried with a loud voice: "Great is the Lord, the God of Daniel." He commanded Daniel to be taken out of the den and the men who had accused him to be thrown in instead. Before these men had reached the bottom, the hungry lions had caught them and broken all their bones.

And the king wrote to all the people of the country: "Fear the God of Daniel, for He is the living and eternal God, and His kingdom shall not be destroyed, and His power shall be forever."

Now answer the following questions:
1. How did Daniel come to Babylon?
2. Why did the king make him governor?
3. Why was Daniel thrown into the lions' den?
4. How did Daniel get food?
5. What happened to the men who accused him?

Daniel was honored by the king because he was a good and wise man. He served his country well, but he knew that he must obey God more than man. God expects us to obey our parents and those who have charge over us. But when they ask us to do what is wrong, we must obey the law of God rather than the law of man.

Daniel was thrown into the lions' den because he prayed to the true God.

The martyrs died because they would not give up their faith in God.

Sometimes even young children have to suffer because they will not offend God by committing sin.

Sin is the greatest evil in the world, because by sin we offend the good God and can lose our souls.

Interesting things for you to do:

1. Read the story of Tarcisius or some other martyr who obeyed the Law of God more than the law of man. Tell the story to the class.

2. Tell the class how the first sin was committed.

3. Can you find or think of another man whom you have read about in this book who was thrown into a pit and whom God protected in a wonderful way afterwards? Read the story again and see in how many ways the two men are alike.

4. Write in your character book: "I must keep away from sin because sin is the greatest evil in the world."

Good things for you to read:

"The Care of God," *Catholic National Reader*, Book IV, page 57.

"Old Nancy's Lesson," *Catholic National Reader*, Book IV, page 90.

"Daniel," *Catholic Youth Reader*, Book IV, page 74.

"Daniel Explains the King's Dream," *The Bible Story*, page 129.

Can you answer the following questions?

1. What is sin?
2. When do we commit sin?
3. In how many ways can we commit sin?
4. What kind of sin do we commit when we offend God in an important matter?
5. What do we lose through mortal sin?
6. How can we keep away from sin?
7. What should we do as soon as we have committed a mortal sin?

58. Saved by a Queen

When the seventy years of captivity were over, the Jews were once more allowed to go back to their own country. However, many of them wanted to stay in Babylon. Among them was the Jew, Mardochai, and his niece Esther. Esther was brought up by Mardochai because her parents were both dead.

It happened that King Assuerus had the most beautiful girls of the country brought before him so that he might choose one of them to be his queen. Esther was among the girls who appeared before him. As soon as the king saw her, he put a crown upon her head and made her queen, for she was the most beautiful of all.

Now, at this time the king made a man named Aman the ruler in the highest place in the kingdom, next to his own. All those who passed in and out of the palace had to bow their knees before him. Mardochai alone, who always stayed near the gates to watch over Esther, never bowed before him, because he was an Israelite and would not bend his knees to anyone but God. This made Aman so angry that he asked the king to have all the Jews in the whole country put to death on a certain day. The king did not know that Esther belonged to the Jewish people and gave Aman permission to do with them as he pleased.

When Mardochai heard that all the Jews of the country were to be killed, he tore his garments and cried aloud. Then he sent word to Esther that she should go to the king and beg him to save her people. But in those days no one, not even the queen, was allowed to appear before the king without first being called. If anyone came to him without permission, he was at once put to death, unless the king held out his golden scepter to him.

Being very much afraid, Esther asked all the Jews to fast and pray for three days. Then she put on her most beautiful garments and went in to the king. When he saw the queen standing before him, he was much as-

"Do not be afraid, Esther. You shall not die."

tonished. But when he noticed that she was turning pale with fear, he said: "What is the matter, Esther? Do not be afraid. You shall not die, for this law is not made for you, but for all others." And he held out his scepter to her.

Then the queen said: "If it please the king, I ask him and Aman to come to the banquet which I have prepared."

So the king and Aman came to the banquet and the king asked Esther again: "What is it that you wish? Whatever you ask for shall be given to you, even if it were half of my kingdom."

Esther answered: "If I have found favor in the king's sight, and if it please the king to give me what I ask, let him and Aman come to the banquet again tomorrow, and I will tell him what I want."

Aman was happy to be invited to a banquet by a queen. But when he was leaving and saw Mardochai sitting at the gate without even moving before him, he was very angry. He went home and ordered a gibbet to be built on which to hang Mardochai, the Jew.

That night King Assuerus could not sleep. Therefore he commanded that the history of his kingdom be read to him. And they read how at one time Mardochai had discovered that two men were planning to kill the king. When Assuerus heard this he said: "What honor and reward has Mardochai received?"

And they answered: "He has received no reward at all."

Just then Aman was coming in to ask the king if he might order Mardochai to be hanged on the gibbet.

Before he could speak, however, the king asked: "What ought to be done to the man whom the king wishes to honor?"

Aman, thinking that the king meant him, said: "The man whom the king wishes to honor, ought to be dressed in the king's garments and to be set on the king's horse, and to have the royal crown put upon his head. And the king's princes and nobles ought to hold the horse and go through the streets of the city with him saying: 'So shall he be honored whom the king wishes to honor.'"

And the king said: "Go and take the garment and the horse and do all that you have said, to Mardochai the Jew." Aman was very angry, but he had to do as he was told.

At the banquet which the queen gave that day, the king asked again: "What is your request, Esther? Although you ask half of my kingdom, you shall have it."

Then she answered: "If I have found favor in your sight, O King, I ask for my life and that of my people."

"Who is it," the king asked, "who wishes to take your life and that of your people?"

And Esther answered: "It is this Aman, our most wicked enemy."

When Aman heard what Esther had said, he could not look into the faces of the king and queen.

Then the king called his servants, and they told him about the gibbet which Aman had built for Mardochai. And the king said to them: "Hang him upon it."

And Aman was hanged on the same gibbet which he had built for Mardochai.

Now answer the following questions:

1. Who was one of the Jews that stayed in Babylon after the captivity was over?
2. Why did he raise the girl Esther?
3. Why did the king choose Esther as queen?
4. What place did Aman hold in the kingdom?
5. What did all the people have to do when Aman passed by? Who refused to bow to Aman? What did Aman want to do to all the Jews?
6. Who saved the Jews from death?
7. How was Aman punished?

Esther loved her country so much that she was willing to risk her life to save her people.

Even young boys and girls have at times helped to save their country. Do you know any story of brave boys and girls who did something for their country?

We cannot all do great things to show our love for our country, but we can do many, many small things, and so get ready for the great things that may be waiting for us in the future.

What great men do you know who have done brave deeds for our country?

What great women do you know who have done brave deeds?

Interesting things for you to do:

1. Appoint a committee to prepare a patriotic program. Some of the boys might tell short stories of their favorite heroes. Be sure to sing a song about your country and find as many pa-

triotic poems as you can to post on the bulletin board or use in the program.

2. Draw an American flag and under it write: "My flag and your flag."

3. Dramatize one of the stories you have read for this lesson.

4. Cut a silhouette of Washington or Lincoln and paste it on a good sheet of paper. Under the picture write a few sentences about him.

5. Read the story of St. George and the Dragon (*A Child's Garden of Religion Stories,* page 231) and draw a picture for it.

6. Read about St. Joan of Arc and tell the class how she saved her country.

Good things for you to read:

"The Fearless Saint," *Wonder Stories,* page 231.

"The Shepherdess Whose Dream Came True," *American Fourth Reader,* page 42.

"Commodore John Barry," *Catholic Youth Reader,* Book IV, page 200.

"The Indians and the Jack-O'-Lanterns," *Misericordia Reader,* Book IV, page 213.

"An Adventure in War Time," *Misericordia Reader,* Book IV, page 225.

"America the Beautiful," *Misericordia Reader,* Book IV, page 240.

"Father Marquette, God's Adventurer," *Misericordia Reader,* Book IV, page 245.

"Nahum Prince," *American Cardinal,* Book IV, page 172.

"A Song for Flag Day," *Cathedral Reader,* Book IV.

"A Story of the Flag," *Cathedral Reader,* Book IV.

"Lord Cornwallis' Knee-Buckles," *Cathedral Reader,* Book IV.

"A Glimpse of Washington," *Cathedral Reader,* Book IV.

"Some Glimpses of Lincoln," *Cathedral Reader,* Book IV.

"How Theodore Roosevelt Overcame His Handicap," *Cathedral Reader*, Book IV.

Can you answer the following questions?

1. Why would Mardochai not bend his knee before Aman?
2. What commandment tells to us that we must adore God alone?
3. How can we adore God?
4. What does the first commandment forbid?

59. A Woman of Courage

The King of Ninive sent Holofernes, the general of his armies, to capture the cities of the Jews. Holofernes marched against the city of Bethulia, and when he saw that the Jews would not surrender, he cut off all the water supply from the city. Soon the people were dying of thirst. Therefore they gathered together before the ruler of the city and said: "Let us give ourselves up to Holofernes, for it is better to live as captives than to see our wives and children die before our eyes."

But he said: "Have courage, my brethren, and let us wait for five days more for mercy from the Lord. But if after five days there is no help, we will give ourselves up to the enemy."

Now there lived in Bethulia a widow named Judith, who was very beautiful. She fasted every day and lived in the fear of the Lord. When she heard what the ruler had said, she sent for some of the men of the city and said: "Who are you, that you tempt the Lord? You have set a time for the Lord and have appointed a day for Him to show His mercy. But the Lord is patient. Let us do penance and with tears ask His pardon."

The men answered: "What you say is true. Pray for us, for you are a holy woman and one fearing God."

Judith said to them: "What I have said comes from God. Tonight I will go out of the city with my servant. Do not ask me what I am doing, but pray for me to the Lord our God."

That night Judith dressed in her most beautiful garments and adorned herself with rich ornaments. Then she left the city and went toward the camp of Holofernes. The Assyrian watchmen met her and asked: "Where are you from and where are you going?"

She answered: "I am a daughter of the Hebrews and I wish to see Holofernes, for I have something to tell him."

When Judith was brought before Holofernes, he was delighted with her great beauty. He ordered that she should be brought into a tent where she could sleep, and that she should be allowed to go in and out as she pleased.

After three days Holofernes had a great supper to which Judith was invited. There he drank so much wine that he lay on his bed drunk as he had never been before. When he was fast asleep, Judith stood before his bed and prayed to God for courage and strength. Then

When Holofernes was asleep Judith struck off his head.

A WOMAN OF COURAGE

she took the sword that hung at his bed and struck off his head with two blows. She gave the head to her maid and the two went out of the camp to their own city.

When the people saw her coming, they all ran out to meet her. Then she stood up high and said: "Praise the Lord our God, who has not forsaken them that hope in Him. This night He has killed the enemy by my hand." And she held up the head of Holofernes, saying: "Behold the head of Holofernes, the general of the army of the Assyrians. Give glory to God, because He is good, because His mercy lasts forever."

And they adored the Lord and thanked Him, and they cried out to her: "You are the glory of Jerusalem, you are the joy of Israel, you are the honor of our people."

When the chiefs of the Assyrian army found the body of Holofernes, they were filled with fear and dread. And the Israelites came out of the city and won a great victory over their enemies.

Now answer the following questions:
1. Who was the general of the Assyrian army?
2. Why were the Israelites dying of thirst?
3. What did they want to do?
4. What did Judith tell the people to do?
5. How did she save her people?
6. Which army was defeated?
7. What did the people call Judith because she saved her country?

The people of Bethulia knew that Judith could be trusted to do the right thing for them. They did not ask her any questions when she left the city, for they knew that they could trust her. Judith was reliable. People are reliable when you can be sure that they will do as they should do, without having someone to look after them. Are you reliable?

Ask yourself the following questions:

Do I keep my promises?

Do I stick to the right when others try to make me do wrong?

Do I ask others to help me with my work in an unfair way?

When I am given work to do, can I be depended on to do it well without being told again?

Do I do my own work instead of letting others do it for me?

Can I be depended upon to keep the laws of my country without being watched or told?

Do I say my prayers at the right time when there is no one to remind me?

Do I behave just as well when my teacher is not in the room as I do when she is?

Do I do the things my parents wish me to do just as well when they are not around as when they are?

Do I remember that God sees me no matter where I am?

The following children are reliable. Try to be like them, so that people will always trust you:

1. Tom's parents go out to visit one evening. Tom promises to take good care of his little sister and brother and not to let anything happen to them. Mother does not worry because she knows the boy has always shown himself reliable.

2. Winnie has to walk seven blocks to school. Although she is still a very little girl, her mother lets her cross the car tracks all alone because Winnie is a very reliable girl and can be trusted to stop, look, and listen before she crosses the street.

3. Teacher asks who can bring some seeds to school the next day. Many boys and girls raise their hands. The teacher asks

James to bring them because she knows he can be depended upon not to forget.

4. Mother is busy with company one night. She tells Marie to put the children to bed. Marie gets the children ready and then says their night prayers with them, although mother did not think of telling her to do so. Marie is only nine years old, but her mother is very proud of her because she can always be depended on to do the right thing.

5. Norbert promised his father that he would never again go out with a certain boy who was not good. Norbert's father knows from the past that his boy would rather lose an arm than break a promise. Therefore he believes that Norbert will keep his word.

6. Ben and Dick plan to go on a fishing trip and then tell the teacher they had to work. Ben wants to ask Leo to come along, but Dick says: "Don't ask Leo. You couldn't get him to do a thing like that for the world." Which of the three boys is most reliable?

7. Mrs. Dunne wants a reliable girl to find a woman for her who lives in an out-of-the-way place. Someone says to her: "If you send Agnes, she will probably come back and tell you the woman cannot be found. But if you send Cleo you may be very sure that she will find the place for you, because Cleo always gets what she goes after."

8. Mary's mother is out shopping and doesn't get home as early as she expected. Mary knows her mother will be in a hurry to get supper and without having been told sets the table, puts water on the stove, and gets everything ready that she knows her mother might need.

9. Something has happened in Tim's house. The neighbor children ask him many questions, but Tim can be trusted not to say a word. He knows that his parents would not like him to talk about this matter to anyone outside of the family.

10. Jane and Joan are in school all alone doing some work for Sister. After Sister has left the room, she remembers that she has a letter on her desk which she does not want any child to see. She does not have time to go back for the letter. Jane and Joan see the letter but do not read it. They are honorable girls. They would not touch things that they know are not meant for them.

11. Al is writing a test after school. The teacher is called out and he is left alone in the classroom. Al has a chance to look in his book, but he knows it is wrong to cheat and therefore will not do it.

12. Bert is passing over a bridge just after a heavy rain. He sees the bridge is not safe for heavy traffic and runs as fast as he can to tell the people in the nearest house about it. He gets there just in time to stop a heavy truck from passing over the bridge.

Good things for you to read:

"The Boy Hero of Harlem," *American Reader,* Book IV, page 214.

"A Guard of Honor," *Catholic National Reader,* Book IV, page 15.

"The Bravest in the Regiment," *Catholic National Reader,* Book IV, page 156.

"Two Boys Avert a Wreck," *American Cardinal Reader,* Book IV, page 194.

"Frank and the Air-Mail Pilot," *Cathedral Basic Readers,* Book IV, page 13.

UNIT VIII

Waiting for the King

When Jacob gave his sons the last blessing, he told Juda that the scepter should not pass from his hands until He would come who was the Promised of all nations.

For many hundred years the Jews were ruled by their own kings. Then came the Babylonian king and carried them away into slavery. Seventy years later they were back again, building up their temple and their homes. But the Jews were no longer a strong nation. They did, indeed, make a brave fight for their freedom, and under great leaders like Judas Machabeus, they succeeded for a while. We shall see, however, that the scepter finally passed out of the hands of the Jews forever. That was a sign that soon the Redeemer would come. All who remembered God's wonderful promise looked hopefully ahead.

They were waiting for the King.

An angel helped Judas in battle.

60. The Last Great Leader

After seventy years of captivity in Babylon the Jews were allowed to go back again to their own country. They returned to Jerusalem with great joy and rebuilt the temple and the city. But they did not enjoy peace very long. Other rulers came in and took the throne. Many of them were cruel and even forbade them to keep the laws which God had given them through Moses.

From time to time brave leaders arose and gathered the people together to fight for their country and their rights. One of the last great leaders was Judas, called the Machabee or "Hammerer" on account of his wonderful courage and strength. With a small company of men he went out to meet the enemy of his country. When the soldiers saw a great army coming toward them, however, they became frightened and said: "How shall we, being only a few, fight against so great and strong an army?"

But Judas said: "Do not fear. It makes no difference to God whether He saves us from a few or many. The success of the war does not depend upon the size of the army but on strength coming from heaven." Then he rushed suddenly upon the enemy and defeated them.

After many victories Judas and his army took Jerusalem. When they found the gates of the temple burned and idols set up in the holy places, they tore their garments and cried aloud. Then they set to work to cleanse the temple and build a new altar. They made new vessels of gold and silver and prepared to offer sacrifice. All the people fell upon their faces and adored and blessed God for having delivered them from the enemy and brought them back into the Holy City.

One time after a great battle which Judas fought against the Assyrians, some of the Jews took away gifts from the idols and hid them under their coats. Now it was forbidden by law to take such gifts. Therefore, when the same men were afterwards found dead on the battlefield, Judas knew that God had punished them for their disobedience. The Israelites prayed that the sins of these men might be forgiven, and Judas sent money to Jerusalem to have sacrifice offered for the dead.

After the death of Judas Machabeus, his brothers became leaders of the people. While they ruled, the Israelites remained true to God. But after their deaths the people fell back into their evil ways. In the end they quarreled among themselves and finally called in the Romans to help them. The Romans came and took possession of the country. Then Juda was no longer a kingdom of its own. The scepter had passed out of Juda's hands.

Now answer the following questions:

1. Why was Judas called "The Hammerer"?
2. Why was he not afraid to fight with a small army?
3. What did the Jews do when they saw how Jerusalem looked?

4. How were those men punished who took the gifts from the idols?

5. What did the people and Judas do for them?

The people of Israel prayed that God would forgive the sins of the dead.

Tonight when you say your prayers before going to bed, be sure to remember the Poor Souls in Purgatory.

Can you answer the following questions?

1. What sacrament should they receive who are expected to die?
2. Where does the soul go after death?
3. What is purgatory?
4. Can we do anything while we are on earth, to shorten our purgatory?

61. He Is Coming

When Adam and Eve sinned, they were sent out of Paradise. But God felt sorry for them and promised them a Redeemer. Adam and Eve did not forget this wonderful promise. They told their children about it, and they, in turn, told their children. So the hope of the Redeemer was kept alive among the Chosen People through all the ages.

From time to time God Himself reminded the Israelites of His promise. He told Abraham that in him all nations would be blessed, and He repeated the same promise to Jacob. Later on He spoke to the people through the great prophets who foretold many things about the Messiah.

Often the Israelites proved unfaithful to God, and often, too, God had to punish them for their sins. In time all the nations became very wicked and turned away from the One True God. Only a small number of Israelites remained faithful to Him and remembered the promise which He had made to Adam and Eve and to the great founders of the Jewish nation. These faithful few knew that the time must be very near for the Redeemer to come, for already the scepter had passed out of the hands of Juda. They longed for Him with all their hearts and prayed that God would send the Promised One very soon.

62. Preparing the World for the Redeemer

We have read the history of the Chosen People of God. We must remember, however, that there were many people living in the world at the time when the scepter passed out of the hand of Juda. If we look on the map and find the land of Chanaan, we shall see that it is only a very small part of the world. The Jews were the only people who believed in the One True God in those days. All the others had long ago forgotten Him and adored idols.

We know how the Jews lost their freedom. They called in the Romans to help them settle their quarrels, and the Romans came and took possession of their land. We shall now see how God made use of the Romans to

In a stable, one glorious night, the Redeemer was born.

prepare the way for the coming of the Redeemer. Of course, they were pagans and did not know that God was directing them. They thought only of their own glory. But that is the way God does. He makes use of people to do His work, even though they do not understand that His hand guides them.

The Romans had their beginning in Rome, a small city on the Tiber river, in the country which is now called Italy. From that city they began to spread out farther and farther, until they took possession of all the countries around the Mediterranean sea. When the Jews called on them for help, they had already become a powerful nation, known as the Roman Empire. Under this Empire, all the nations were united. They were governed by one man, who was called the emperor. The first emperor who ruled over the Roman Empire was Julius Cæsar. The second, was Augustus. The different countries belonging to the Roman Empire were ruled by governors appointed by the emperor. The land of the Jews was governed by Herod and Pontius Pilate.

The Romans had built great roads to all parts of the Empire. That made travel easier and safer than ever before. Nearly everybody spoke or at least understood the Latin or the Greek language, which made it possible afterwards to spread the teachings of the Redeemer much faster. The Jews were scattered in different countries and had told others about the One True God and about the expected Redeemer. All the nations were united under one ruler, as we have seen, and the whole world was at peace. Everything was ready to receive the Messiah. Everybody seemed to be waiting for the King who was to come.

Then the Emperor Augustus sent out word that all his people should be counted. Every man was to go to the city of his birth to be enrolled. So it happened that Mary and Joseph left their home in Nazareth and went to the little town of Bethlehem, the city of David, to which they belonged. Here, one glorious night, the Redeemer was born. He was born in a stable, because there was no room in the inn for Mary, His mother, and Joseph, her spouse.

Christ the Redeemer, the Son of God, lived, and preached, and died in Chanaan, the land of His Chosen People. We know that they refused to believe in Him and that they put Him to death. But His teaching spread over the whole earth. It spread more quickly and more easily, because the world was prepared for Him, and all the nations were united under one rule, that of the Roman Empire.

Down through the ages came the teachings of the Redeemer, and we, His children, have taken the place of His Chosen People, the Jews. We have never seen Him face to face, as they saw Him, and we have never heard the music of His voice. But He has left us His Church to teach us the way to Him; and some day, if we love and serve Him, He will call us to live with Him in His Kingdom. And, as the Holy Bible tells us,

"Eye hath not seen nor ear heard, neither hath it

entered into the heart of man, what things God hath prepared for them that love Him."

Now answer the following questions:

1. Who were the only people that believed in the One True God before the Redeemer came?
2. How did the Romans get the land of the Jews?
3. Did the Romans know that God was using them to prepare the way for the Redeemer?
4. Where did the Roman Empire have its beginning?
5. What was the ruler of the Roman Empire called?
6. Who was the second ruler of the Roman Empire?
7. Who were the two governors of the Jews at this time?
8. How was the world prepared for the Redeemer?
9. Why did Mary and Joseph have to go to Bethlehem?
10. In what country did the Redeemer live and die?

Interesting things for you to do:

1. Find the following places on the map: Chanaan, Bethlehem, Mediterranean Sea, Italy, Tiber River, Rome.
2. Tell something about each of the places that you were to find on the map.
3. Read the lesson which tells how David was anointed king and find in what city he lived.
4. Read the lesson about Ruth and find how she was related to David.
5. Tell the class the story of the Wise Men who came to ask Herod about the Redeemer.
6. Tell what you know about Pontius Pilate.
7. The Roman Empire also included the greater part of England, France, Spain, and Germany. Find these countries on the map of Europe.
8. Tell the class how you think each of the following made

the spread of Christ's teachings easier: good roads; one language understood by all; all nations under one ruler; peace in the world; Jews scattered in different countries.

9. Write a list of as many names as you can think of, by which the Redeemer was called.

10. Tell the meaning of the Scripture text at the end of the lesson and then memorize it.

11. In your history book find something about Julius Cæsar or the Founding of Rome and tell the class what you have read.

12. Find out the meaning of Advent, when it is, and how long it lasts.

13. Look on the church calendar for the season of Advent. With what color is it marked? Why?

14. Go back over the stories in this book and find out to how many people the Redeemer was promised.

15. Read over the lessons about the psalms and the prophets and see how many things were foretold about the Redeemer. Can you say any of these texts by heart?

16. Imagine that you are a Jewish boy or girl living in Jerusalem at the time when the Redeemer was expected. A little Roman neighbor asks you about your religion and especially about your hope for the Messiah. Tell the class what you would say to him.

17. Imagine that you are the little Roman boy. Write a letter to your friend in Rome and tell him what you have just found out about the Redeemer.

18. Some of the beautiful hymns that are sung in church during Advent tell of the great longing in the hearts of the people for the Redeemer. Find one of these hymns and read or sing it for the class.

Prayers

The Sign of the Cross

In the name of the Father, and of the Son, and of the Holy Ghost. Amen.

The Our Father

Our Father, Who art in heaven, hallowed be Thy name. Thy kingdom come, Thy will be done on earth as it is in heaven.

Give us this day our daily bread, and forgive us our trespasses as we forgive those who trespass against us. And lead us not into temptation, but deliver us from evil. Amen.

The Hail Mary

Hail, Mary, full of grace, the Lord is with thee. Blessed art thou among women, and blessed is the fruit of thy womb, Jesus.

Holy Mary, Mother of God, pray for us sinners, now and at the hour of our death. Amen.

The Apostles' Creed

I believe in God, the Father Almighty, Creator of heaven and earth. And in Jesus Christ, His only Son, our Lord: Who was conceived by the Holy Ghost, born of the Virgin Mary, suffered under Pontius Pilate, was crucified, died, and was buried. He descended into Hell, the third day He arose from the dead. He ascended into Heaven, sitteth at the right hand of God the Father Almighty. From thence He shall come to judge the living and the dead. I believe in the Holy Ghost, the Holy Catholic Church, the communion of saints, the forgiveness of sins, the resurrection of the body, and life everlasting. Amen.

An Act of Faith

O my God! I firmly believe that Thou art one God in three Divine Persons, Father, Son, and Holy Ghost. I believe that Thy Divine Son became man, and died for our sins, and that He will come to judge the living and the dead. I believe these and all the truths which the Holy Catholic Church teaches, because Thou hast revealed them, Who canst neither deceive nor be deceived.

An Act of Hope

O my God! Relying on Thy infinite goodness and promises, I hope to obtain pardon of my sins, the help of Thy Grace, and life everlasting, through the merits of Jesus Christ, my Lord and Redeemer.

An Act of Charity, or Love

O my God! I love Thee above all things, with my whole heart and soul, because Thou art all-good and worthy of all love. I love my neighbor as myself, for love of Thee. I forgive all who have injured me, and ask pardon of all whom I have injured.

An Act of Contrition

O my God! I am heartily sorry for having offended Thee, and I detest all my sins, because I dread the loss of heaven and the pains of hell, but most of all because they offend Thee, my God, Who art all-good and deserving of all my love. I firmly resolve with the help of Thy grace, to confess my sins, to do penance, and to amend my life.

The Confiteor, or I Confess

I confess to Almighty God, to blessed Mary ever Virgin, to blessed Michael the Archangel, to blessed John the Baptist, to the holy Apostles Peter and Paul, and to all the saints, that I have sinned exceedingly in thought, word, and deed, *through my fault, through my fault, through my most grievous fault.* Therefore, I beseech blessed Mary ever Virgin, blessed Michael the Archangel, blessed John the Baptist, the holy Apostles Peter and Paul, and all the saints, to pray to the Lord our God for me.

May the Almighty God have mercy on me, forgive me my sins, and bring me to everlasting life. Amen.

May the Almighty and Merciful Lord grant me pardon, absolution, and remission of all my sins. Amen.

The Glory be to the Father

Glory be to the Father, and to the Son, and to the Holy Ghost. As it was in the beginning, is now, and ever shall be, world without end. Amen.

Prayer to the Guardian Angel

Angel of God, my guardian dear,
   To whom His love commits me here,
Ever this day be at my side
   To light, to guard, to rule and guide.
                         Amen.

The Angelus

(At morning, noon, and night)

V. The angel of the Lord declared unto Mary.
R. And she conceived of the Holy Ghost.
   Hail Mary, etc.
V. Behold the handmaid of the Lord.
R. Be it done unto me according to Thy word
   Hail Mary, etc.
V. And the Word was made flesh.
R. And dwelt among us.
   Hail Mary, etc.
V. Pray for us, O holy Mother of God.
R. That we may be made worthy of the promises of Christ.

Blessing Before Meals

Bless us, O Lord, and these Thy gifts, which we are about to receive from Thy bounty, through Christ our Lord. Amen.

Thanksgiving After Meals

We return Thee thanks, Almighty God, for these Thy benefits, which we have received from Thy bounty, through Christ, our Lord. Amen.

Prayer Before a Crucifix

A plenary indulgence may be gained after Confession and Holy Communion by *saying* this prayer before a crucifix or a picture of one. Granted by Pope Pius IX, July 31, 1858.

Behold, O kind and most sweet Jesus, I cast myself on my knees in Thy sight, and with the most fervent desire of my soul I pray and beseech Thee to fix deep in my soul lively sentiments of faith, hope, and charity, with true repentance for my sins, and a firm desire of amendment, while with deep love and grief of soul I ponder within myself and mentally contemplate Thy five most precious wounds; having before my eyes that which David spoke in prophecy: "They have pierced My Hands and My Feet; they have numbered all My Bones."

Say some prayers for the intention of the Holy Father.

Ejaculations

Eternal rest give unto them, O Lord, and let perpetual light shine upon them.

Sweet Heart of Jesus, be my love.

O Lord, my God, in Thee have I put my trust: save me from all them that persecute me and deliver me (Ps. vii).

Blessed art Thou, O Lord the God of our fathers; and worthy to be praised, and glorified, and exalted above all for ever: and blessed is the holy name of Thy glory: and worthy to be praised, and exalted above all in all ages (Dan. iii. 52).

Prayers for Communion
(From the Catechism of Pius X)
Before Communion
Faith

My Lord Jesus Christ, I firmly believe that Thou art truly present with Thy Body and Blood, Thy soul and divinity in the Most Holy Sacrament of the Eucharist.

Adoration

O Lord, I adore Thee in this Sacrament and confess that Thou art my Maker, my Redeemer and supreme Lord, and my greatest and only Good.

Humility

O Lord, I am not worthy that Thou shouldst enter under my roof; but say only the word and my soul shall be healed.

Sorrow

O Lord, I detest all my sins because they have made me unworthy to receive Thee into my heart. I resolve, with the help of Thy grace, not to commit these sins in the future, to avoid their occasions, and to do penance for them.

Hope

O Lord, I hope that Thou wilt give me Thyself entirely in this divine Sacrament; that Thou wilt show me Thy mercy and give me all the graces that I need for my salvation.

Love

O my Lord, Thou art infinitely worthy of all love; Thou art my Father, my Saviour, and my God! therefore I love

Thee with my whole heart more than all other things, I love also my neighbor as myself, for love of Thee. I forgive all who have injured me.

Desire

O Lord, I desire greatly that Thou should come into my heart. I will never part from Thee, and I will live always in Thy grace.

After Communion

Faith

My Lord Jesus Christ, I believe that Thou art truly present within me, with Thy Body and Blood, soul and divinity; I believe it more firmly than if I saw it with my own eyes.

Adoration

O my Jesus, I adore Thee, because Thou art present within me. I join myself with the Blessed Virgin Mary, and with the angels and saints, in order to adore Thee as Thou deservest.

Thanks

O Jesus, my Lord, I thank Thee with my whole heart, for coming to me. Holy Virgin Mary, my guardian angel, and you saints and angels of heaven, thank Jesus for me.

Love

O Jesus my God, I love Thee with all my love. I wish to love Thee as much as Thou deservest; give me the grace to love Thee above all things, now and through all eternity.

Offering

O my Jesus; Thou hast given me all; see, I too will give Thee all: I offer Thee my heart and my soul. I consecrate my whole life to Thee, and I will belong to Thee for all eternity.

Hope

O my Jesus! Thou hast come into my heart. I hope that Thou wilt never separate Thyself from me, but always stay with me through Thy divine grace.

Petition

O my Jesus! Give me, I beg Thee, all those spiritual and temporal graces which will be helpful to my soul. Help my parents, my superiors, my friends, benefactors, and the poor souls in Purgatory. Amen.

Ejaculations

Lord, Thou knowest that I love Thee.

May the Body and Blood of our Lord Jesus Christ preserve my soul to everlasting life.

My Jesus mercy! Save me by Your Precious Blood.

Jesus, in the Most Holy Sacrament, have mercy on us.

I will give praise to Thee, O Lord, with my whole heart (Ps. ix).

Preserve me, O Lord, for I have put my trust in Thee (Ps. xv).

My God *is* my helper, and in Him will I put my trust (Ps. xvii).

To Thee, O Lord, have I lifted up my soul. In Thee, O my God, I put my trust, let me not be ashamed (Ps. xxiv).

I will bless the Lord at all times. His praise shall be always in my mouth (Ps. xxxiii).

Forsake me not, O Lord my God: do not Thou depart from me. Attend unto my help, O Lord, the God of my salvation (Ps. xxxvii).

And now, O Lord, think of me, and take not revenge of my sins, neither remember my offenses nor those of my parents (Tob. iii. 3).

The Rosary

The Joyful Mysteries

On Mondays, Thursdays, and on the Sundays from Advent to Lent:

The Angel Gabriel announces to the Blessed Virgin that she is to be the Mother of Jesus
The Virgin Mary visits her cousin Elizabeth
The birth of our Lord Jesus Christ
The presentation of Jesus in the Temple
The finding of Jesus in the Temple

The Sorrowful Mysteries

On Tuesdays, Fridays, and on the Sundays of Lent:
The agony of Jesus in the garden
The scourging of Jesus at the pillar
The crowning of Jesus with thorns
Jesus carries His cross
The crucifixion

The Glorious Mysteries

On Wednesdays, Saturdays, and on the Sundays from Easter to Advent:

The resurrection of Jesus from the dead
The ascension of Jesus into heaven
The descent of the Holy Ghost upon the Apostles
The assumption (taking) of the Blessed Virgin into heaven
The crowning of the Blessed Virgin as Queen of Heaven

Stations of the Cross

Say the Act of Contrition.

Before each station, genuflect and say:

We adore Thee, O Christ, and bless Thee. Because by Thy holy cross Thou hast redeemed the world.

After each station, say:
Lord Jesus Crucified, have mercy on us.

First Station, Jesus is Condemned to Death
Second Station, Jesus Carries His Cross
Third Station, Jesus Falls the First Time Under His Cross
Fourth Station, Jesus Meets His Blessed Mother
Fifth Station, Simon of Cyrene Helps Jesus to Carry the Cross
Sixth Station, Veronica Wipes the Face of Jesus
Seventh Station, Jesus Falls the Second Time Under the Cross
Eighth Station, Jesus Speaks to the Women
Ninth Station, Jesus Falls the Third Time
Tenth Station, Jesus is Stripped of His Garments
Eleventh Station, Jesus is Nailed to the Cross
Twelfth Station, Jesus Dies on the Cross
Thirteenth Station, Jesus is Taken Down From the Cross
Fourteenth Station, Jesus is Laid in the Sepulcher

Ejaculations

Jesus, Mary, Joseph.
Jesus, Mary, Joseph, I give You my heart and soul.
Infant Jesus, bless us.
Blessed be God.
Jesus, my God, I love Thee above all things.
My Lord and my God.
O sweet Heart of Jesus, I implore, that I may ever love thee more and more.
Jesus, meek and humble of heart, make my heart like unto Thine.
Jesus, I adore Thee.
Blessed be Jesus Christ, true God and true Man.
Blessed be the great Mother of God, Mary most holy.
Let us give thanks to the Lord, our God.

www.ingramcontent.com/pod-product-compliance
Lightning Source LLC
Chambersburg PA
CBHW050928240426
43671CB00019B/2955